DES
O'MALLEY
a political profile

DES O'MALLEY
a political profile

Dick Walsh

BRANDON

Published by Brandon Book Publishing Ltd.,
Dingle, Co. Kerry, Ireland;
and 27 South Main Street, Dover, New Hampshire 03894-2069, USA.

British Library Cataloguing in Publication Data

Walsh, Dick
    Des O'Malley: a political profile.
    1. O'Malley, Des   2. Politicians —
    Ireland — Biography
    I. Title
    941.70824'092'4   DA965.04/

ISBN 0-86322-087-8

Cover design by Paula Nolan

Printed by Richard Clay plc

Contents

Why O'Malley?

WHY O'MALLEY? First, because he became so suddenly the joker in the pack: a month after he and Mary Harney formed the Progressive Democrats in December 1985 the party had won the support of one-fifth of the electorate. Within three months, it was ahead of Fine Gael, the senior partner in an increasingly hard-pressed Coalition, and although its ratings in the opinion polls seemed to settle down somewhere between 13 and 17 per cent, the major parties viewed this new phenomenon with continuing unease — O'Malley had not just carved a niche for himself; he had filled a space which their catch-all organisations and policies had allowed to grow.

How and why this happened is the second, and perhaps more important, reason for examining his career; for his sudden popularity asked as many questions as it answered about Ireland in the Eighties. Though he and his new party said much about breaking the mould of Civil War politics, it was not as simple as that; nor was it merely a case of bringing to political leadership that combination of surefooted efficiency and patent integrity which people thought lacking in the other senior contenders for their loyalty. The nature of his appeal lay not so much in a new variation of the presidential style that had become common to the leaders of Fianna Fáil and Fine Gael since the Seventies as in an ability and willingness to articulate views which these leaders had chosen to ignore.

One of O'Malley's old sparring partners, Conor Cruise O'Brien, attended the new party's first national conference in May. He had already decided that its leader's personality had mellowed with the years; as he said, "a new gravitas tinged with melancholy" had entered his soul. True, O'Malley had come to adopt a cool, slightly ironic tone where once he had sounded arrogant and behaved aggressively. Now, O'Brien noted the "rasping crackle that comes out with a subliminal effect of menace from under the softness natural to the Limerick speech" but he added admiringly: "You can't listen to him, these days, without feeling that this might be a difficult man to stop." That appealed to O'Brien, if only because the man he wanted stopped was an older and even hungrier enemy than O'Malley, Charlie Haughey.

These changes, too, are noteworthy though of less significance than the evolution of O'Malley's attitude to social and national issues. How, for instance, has the man who once declared it a legislator's duty to discourage fornication come

2

to the conclusion that standing by the Republic means adopting a liberal approach to contraception, divorce and women's affairs? How does the argument that Ireland is one because God made it so sit with the view that those who clamour for unity are engaged in an exercise in futility? And by what route did the proponent of orthodoxy in social and national affairs arrive at the conclusion that the separation of Church and State was essential to the functioning of a modern democracy?

O'Malley's views on financial and economic matters have changed less over the years than his opinions on social issues. They are, however, in some respects more controversial: approached with deep suspicion and considerable hostility by politicians of the Left who would readily agree with him on contraception, divorce or Church-State relations; firmly shared by some supporters who feel slightly uneasy with his progressive social line. Garret FitzGerald was the first of many observers to place the PDs in the classic tradition of European liberals: strongly opposed to intervention by the State in any area. Labour, the Workers' Party and even some members of Fianna Fáil are convinced that, given the opportunity, the party would dismantle as much of the State apparatus as possible, removing the protection of a welfare system that has been painstakingly constructed and selling off resources, natural and industrial, to allow for wholesale cuts in public spending and taxes, renewed stimulation for private enterprise.

The PDs' critics on the Left thought they detected more fur coats, certainly fewer open-necked shirts, among the audiences that poured into halls throughout the country in the spring of '86. They were bigger audiences than any politician had managed to muster for decades. They were also more enthusiastic and many, perhaps most, of them had never had a hand in politics before. "Amateurs," growled the old pros in Fianna Fáil. "The kind of people who go out to vote," according to worried activists in Fine Gael. They were, indeed, fired by a missionary zeal. No one would have been surprised if they had joined hands and sung charismatic hymns.

But there were more of them than there were at the rallies which Fianna Fáil mounted as a counter-attraction. And as seasoned observers talked about the middle classes in revolt, attention began to be focussed on the extent of the class or classes to which O'Malley and his party gave voice, the depth of the frustrations and ambitions which other politicians had clearly failed to represent. Within weeks of setting up shop in South Frederick Street, the PDs had twice as many members as the Labour Party; within months, it was said, as much money in their funds as would account for over 65 per cent of a Fianna Fáil national collection. Long before the summer recess the party's parliamentary group, with former members of Fianna Fáil, Fine Gael and Labour, was fourth in size in the Oireachtas and if it did not hold the balance of power it was too close to that position for the comfort of anyone who feared the imminence of a General Election.

The major parties had every reason to be worried. Not since 1969 had a government been re-elected although, with the exception of 1977, there had been no dramatic change in Dáil representation. In 1981 and the first election of 1982, administrations had been left hanging on the support of minority groups or Independents, proving that the electorate, far from showing the volatility which many had predicted, may have been dissatisfied with Tweedledum's performance but was unwilling to hand power to Tweedledee. There was more and more talk of problems that appeared intractable:

the North, unemployment, the level of the current budget deficit, a high dependency ratio and the bruising weight of taxation.

A society which had welcomed industrialisation in the Sixties and EEC membership in the Seventies was proving unwilling or unable to come to terms with its new, urban personality and its vulnerability to outside influences. Twice in three years what the political scientist, Tom Garvin, called the politics of cultural defence came to the fore with a vengeance. Two referenda exposed a popular reluctance to meet the challenge of modernising Church-State relations. On both occasions, reforming politicians were seen to come off second-best to a combination of clerical and lay fundamentalist forces. The EEC, when it was not being regarded as an ever ready source of funds, was looked upon as an absentee landlord of sorts, remote, greedy and essentially indifferent to Irish needs.

There were bitter economic disappointments. Multinational companies which had been welcomed with open arms, generous grants and even more generous tax incentives in the Sixties and Seventies simply upped and left, even when their Irish operations were profitable, as the recession forced retrenchment or newer pastures offered sweeter terms. Long established Irish companies, priced out of their markets abroad or unable to stand the heat of foreign competition at home, unceremoniously closed their doors. Economists blamed politicians for keeping State-supported white elephants alive; and trade unions blamed them for allowing white elephants, State-supported or otherwise, to die.

As unemployment climbed, middle-aged people who would never work again joined the young who had never had the chance to work in an apparently hopeless round of futility and frustration. It was not an experience confined to Ireland, as many discovered when emigration, the nightmare of the Fifties, started once more. But it seemed more cruel, maybe because Ireland had come late to the post-war boom and now, at last, had a youthful and by and large well educated population. Unemployment bred poverty and poverty bred crime. But it was among the least educated, the least skilled, that the cycle was most difficult to break; children trapped in their parents' deprivation. And as poverty bred crime, crime bred resentment — among those who felt threatened by unemployment or, perhaps more so, by the unemployed.

Conservative politicians had taken it in turn for more than a decade to issue warnings of the risk of upheaval among those who were most deprived. They saw the threat coming from the Left, whose organisations, it was thought, would find rich recruiting grounds in the dole queues. They foresaw a particular problem with the young. The worrying thing about the challenge of the PDs, viewed from the opposite sides of Mount Street on which Fianna Fáil and Fine Gael have their headquarters, was that it came neither from the Left nor, for the most part, from the very young but from people who, with the odd exception, would not have been out of place in Fianna Fáil or Fine Gael.

O'Malley refuses to assemble his supporters under any flag of convenience, arguing that the labels of class are points on a British political compass and are irrelevant in Irish conditions; such expressions as Left and Right are simply alien. John Kelly of Fine Gael has noted how the words alien and ideology tend to be linked in Irish minds; Labour and the Workers' Party would claim that in O'Malley's case the link is automatic and almost always applies to the Left. He is adamant that the Right-wing label is equally distasteful.

Are there echoes here of an old Fianna Fáil claim — ''we are neither servants of the Right, nor prisoners of the Left but pragmatists of the Centre" — which Haughey produced in 1982 to justify a catch-all appeal? Is O'Malley in the business of being all things to all men (and women) — as Fianna Fáil certainly once was and still aspires to be, or as Fine Gael under FitzGerald became for a time and might still have been, had not the pressures of cultural defence and financial orthodoxy returned to haunt that party as nationalism in the late Sixties returned to haunt Fianna Fáil? O'Malley says "No." His constituency, even if he does not care to put labels on it, is more narrowly defined. Nor does he care for comparison with Clann na Poblachta, the last new party to have had an impact on Irish politics.

There are, however, some points of similarity between the Progressive Democrats and Clann na Poblachta. Clann, too, benefited from disillusion with Fianna Fáil and, winning two out of three by-elections in the autumn of 1947, got off to a good start. So good that its organisers decided, unwisely as it happened, to put up two candidates in each constituency in the 1948 General Election. Taking over 13 per cent of the first preference votes, they won 10 seats and joined an Inter-Party Government with Fine Gael, Labour, Clann na Talmhan and Independents.

But, as Ronan Fanning writes in his book *Independent Ireland*, Clann na Poblachta

> advocated a more active campaign against Partition and favoured admitting the electoral representatives of the Catholic minority in Northern Ireland to the Oireachtas. They also laid heavy emphasis on social issues and attacked the evils of emigration, unemployment and rising prices... indeed, their emphasis on social issues was sufficiently radical for Fianna Fáil, now a bastion of respectability and vested interests, to see nothing incongruous in turning against Clann candidates that same "red scare" tactic used

against its own candidates in 1932-33. Above all the Clann sought to take advantage of the post-war disillusion with a joyless government and to capitalise on the stale sense of weariness produced by 16 years in office.

When he was asked about comparison with Clann O'Malley quickly issued a disclaimer:

Clann na Poblachta was a relatively radical party, drawn from one end of the political spectrum. We are much more in the centre of things. Because they tended towards one end of the spectrum, they drew support only from people who approximated to that position. With us it's different. We are drawing on the support of all parties.

So the PDs lay no claim to radicalism; nor is their argument with Fianna Fáil what Fanning called the perennial argument about who is the better Republican — not at any rate in the sense in which it was the issue between Sean MacBride and Eamon de Valera. In the dispute between the founders of Clann na Poblachta and Fianna Fáil, O'Malley would, if anything, find himself closer to Dev. And the parallels with Dev's New Departure?

Fianna Fáil was founded in reaction to the Civil War — its founders opposed those, the majority in Sinn Féin, who were saying essentially that the Civil War should continue. There is a parallel now, inasmuch as we would seem very much to be beginning to confront our own problems in the context of the present and future rather than in the context of the past — the old Civil War divisions and so on.

In truth, the problems of the present have more to do with the changes of the last 20 years than with anything else. It is a period of transition that cannot yet be tidied up and filed away with convenient conclusions. But a look at O'Malley's origins and development may help to unravel the story so far.

Dynasty

DES O'MALLEY SHRUGS off the suggestion of a dynasty; but before he ever thought of entering politics his family had reached an uncommonly powerful position in Limerick. His father, also called Des, and two of his uncles, Michael and Donogh, had served as mayors of the city. Des senior, in particular, was a highly valued member of Fianna Fáil, although long after his death stories persisted about how he could as easily have stood for Fine Gael. Both Eamon de Valera and Sean Lemass pressed him to accept the nomination when the patriarchal Limerick Republican, Dan Burke, who had been in the Dáil since the Twenties, died in 1952. When he refused, the offer passed after a short delay to Donogh. Des was to remain Fianna Fáil's anchor man in the constituency while Donogh became one of Lemass's mohair-suited men and, in time, one of the most adventurous and innovative Ministers in the history of the State.

Some politicians find themselves stretching a tenuous line of kinship to make a connection with the constituency they hope to represent. Des O'Malley bore the indelible stamp of his family; and the O'Malleys were quintessentially Limerick.

The first thing that most Limerick people will tell you about their city is that it is not as outsiders see it: ultra-conservative, pious and poor. O'Malley is no exception. To him, the city is — outside Dublin — the most cosmopolitan place in the country. And there's no denying that from the settlement of the 17th century to the development of Shannon in the 1950s, Limerick has been exposed to regular, if sometimes unwelcome, doses of outside influence. It was here, after the cruel sieges of 1690 and 1691, that the Wild Geese spread their wings; and the garrison that replaced them, with a broken treaty and wounded pride, stood guard over a new order. Gaelic Ireland died in Limerick, Irish troops went to fight on "far foreign fields" and the Williamite forces consolidated their success which, as the English historian, G. M. Trevelyan, noted, marked a turning point in European history.

In Limerick the new settlers — and, indeed, many of the old as well — welcomed the garrison and felt grateful for its protection. Merchants and tradespeople took the living that it provided and asked no questions. But others saw in it a bitter reminder of an old betrayal, a humiliating memorial to a cause that seemed forever lost until, in one of the fiercest struggles of the War of Independence, the garrison was dispatched in 1922. Limerick was, and still is, to a great extent, a city of layers.

Even in the centuries after the broken treaty, its prosperity grew. Not that everyone enjoyed it: in the 1770s, for example, the poor of the city laid siege to its flour mills and had to be fought off by the militia. But for the settlers and merchants life was full of delights. They made the most of what the poet, Spencer, had called "The spacious Shenan spreading like the sea." Upriver, they took the air by the falls of Doonass or across the weir at Castleconnell, where they built a discreet and elegant resort. They ventured downstream on boats owned by an ancestor of the actor, Richard Harris, that plied between the city, Foynes, Tarbert and Kilrush, from where it was a short, overland spin to the seaside at Kilkee. On their journey they passed the scene of that recent ghastly drowning of a young girl by a paid murderer. Gerald Griffin, a reporter on the *Chronicle*, had made a book of it called *The Collegians*. The book was to be turned into a melodrama, *The Colleen Bawn* (Ah dear Mr. Boucciccault) and an opera, *The Lily of Killarney*. They had theatres and music-halls on their doorsteps. That, at least, was something the rest of the citizens could enjoy: when O'Mara, the tenor, returned to the city from a triumphant European tour, thousands turned up to stand beneath the balcony of his hotel in Bedford Row to hear him sing. Everyone could recite "Drunken Thady and the Bishop's Lady" by their own Bard of Thomond, Michael Hogan, though few enough probably knew of the works of Brian Merriman of Clare who completed his masterly satire *The Midnight Court* while teaching mathematics in the city.

A city of layers, indeed. To this day, the huddled streets and lanes of The Parish (St. Mary's) are a world away from

11

the spreading lawns of Castletroy or the solid brick of the Ennis road. And there are lines of local geography which the outsider will pass without noticing: a corner turned, a bridge crossed and there is a new inflexion, a new tone which only the most finely tuned ear in a musically inclined city will detect.

The change of tone is often more than musical: tuppence-ha'penny looking down on tuppence is one local version of the many social distinctions which are entwined in the barely perceptible boundaries. "Old stock" is a commendation that money can't buy. Lineage and schools are important to the status-conscious. And games, or at any rate rugby: Limerick is one of the few cities in Ireland where rugby has a strong working class following. This, however, does not mean that the working class players join the professional and propertied men who, elsewhere, are most commonly associated with the game. The working classes have their own clubs, Shannon and Young Munster; the middle classes play with Garryowen; the well-to-do join Bohemians and Old Crescent. Each group has its meeting places; members rarely break into each other's territory.

The O'Malleys fit comfortably into this urban maze. Not in the top layer, but near enough. They are long enough resident to be considered "old stock". Des O'Malley's paternal grandfather was an architect; his maternal grandfather owned a hotel. Their children were educated by the Jesuits at the Crescent or by the Faithful Companions of Jesus at Laurel Hill. They were, as Limerick puts it, cut out for the professions. Donogh played his rugby with Bohemians and, if it hadn't been for the war, might have been capped for Ireland. Given the circumstances that prevailed once independence had been achieved, they were the kind of people that might naturally be expected to have had a hand in running the affairs of the new State.

Des O'Malley was born in Eden Terrace on the North Circular Road in 1939. He was three when his parents moved back to his father's old home where Corbally slopes gently towards the river. It may not have been the city's most exclusive area, but they had the Catholic Bishop of Limerick for a neighbour. For Des, his sister Denise and brothers Joseph and Peter, school lay on the other side of the city. To get there they passed through The Parish and the city centre; and there were five Catholic churches along the way. Through the Forties and the Fifties, neither the city''s poverty nor its piety could be ignored.

"It was only 15 years earlier that the first slum clearances took place," O'Malley now recalls. "Slums were still very visible even around the centre of the city. I think everyone had to be conscious of them. And remember, welfare levels were very low, not just by comparison with what they are now, but in absolute terms." As for religion, it was a dominant influence in everyone's lives. These were the heydays of the Arch Confraternity of the Holy Family which claimed a membership of ten thousand men and boys. O'Malley himself never joined but served Mass regularly at the Jesuit church down the road from the Redemptorists' where the Arch Confraternity met to wage war on the devil with all his works and pomps. It was about this time that a group of Jehovah's Witnesses was set upon by a gang of men near Killaloe in Co. Clare: and when the case was heard in Limerick it was the Witnesses who were bound to the peace.

At home in Corbally, however, the talk was of politics and books. It was a busy house. O'Malley senior was the eldest of a family of twelve and considered himself responsible for his brothers and sisters as well as for his own children.

Donogh, whether in college or later in politics, often brought his troubles to be sorted out. A brother-in-law, Stan Stewart, and his wife, Nora, brought news of the world of art and literature. Occasionally they were accompanied by a tall grey-haired man called O'Donovan: he turned out to be the writer, Frank O'Connor. And there were frequent visits from Gerry O'Brien whose sister, Kate O'Brien, had lately been banned for half a sentence in an otherwise irreproachable novel. The family kept a lookout for the works of Sean O'Faolain, Liam O'Flaherty and others lest all of Frank O'Mahony's copies be snapped up before he was forced to remove them from the shelves of his bookshop in O'Connell Street.

Lemass phoned regularly, probably about once a month, to seek advice. Dev also called, especially when he was trying to convince O'Malley senior that he should stand in the by-election. To Lemass he was a valuable sounding board, one of several throughout the country who could be relied upon to give a straightforward answer to a straightforward question. An observer who had watched him during the last years of his career in local government said: "It might take him some time to make up his mind, but when his mind was made up, he didn't mince his words. You knew all about it."

Perhaps because his father had already suffered a heart attack and had a big legal practice to look after, it was taken for granted that Des should follow in his professional footsteps. He came to take it for granted early on. Certainly, no thought of an active career in politics entered his head; Donogh, after all, was the full-time politician in the family. Indeed, the only political event that seems to have impinged deeply on his consciousness at the time — the end of the Fifties — was the funeral of Sean South, a Limerick man shot during the IRA campaign. He had become something of a folk hero almost before his body had been brought home

Donogh O'Malley with Mrs Seán MacEntee outside Leinster House, April 1965. Irish Times

to Limerick. O'Malley was among the thousands who attended the funeral. They had known each other slightly, since South was a regular communicant at the Jesuit church:

It had quite an effect. He was someone, however misguided he may have been, that you couldn't but help feel was in the same tradition as, perhaps, those of 1916 and 1921. He was a gentleman, very much a Christian in the true sense of the word and, in the proper sense, he was a soldier — he had the kind of qualities one would look for in a real soldier as opposed to a terrorist or a gangster. That explains the different attitude that could have been taken then to South and some of the other people involved in their very limited campaign by comparison with the present set-up where you don't have people of that calibre or quality at all but, by and large, thugs who engage in atrocities by any standard. Yes, I was aware of the type of man that he was, a dignified man and a Christian type of man.

These sentiments, however qualified, must sound surprising, especially to those who viewed O'Malley simply in the light of his performance as Minister for Justice — the youngest and arguably the toughest since Kevin O'Higgins. But Irish politics are never as simple as they seem and O'Malley's family, too, has had its share of wartime tragedy. On 19 April 1921, his mother's father, Denis O'Donovan, was shot dead by British Auxiliaries in his hotel at Castleconnell. It appears that IRA men from Clare and Limerick were using the weir to cross the river and meeting in the hotel bar. The incident is described by Charles Townshend in his book *The British Campaign in Ireland, 1919-1921.*

The raiding force, commanded by Capt./2nd D.I. Wood, was divided into two parties. Two officers and twelve cadets in plain clothes were ordered to filter unobtrusively into the hotel bar to look for suspects, while a uniformed party of an officer and twenty cadets with two Lewis guns surrounded the area. As they drove up to Castleconnell, however, a number of men were seen running across the fields, and the Auxiliaries promptly forgot their plans.

The plainclothes party, on reaching the hotel, rushed straight into the bar, shouting "Hands Up!" In the bar were three off duty RIC men, who took the intruders to be rebels, opened fire on them, and drove them out. A brisk exchange followed in which an RIC sergeant in the bar and a cadet in the courtyard outside were killed.

Eventually the arrival of the uniformed party led the two remaining RIC men in the bar to realise the mistake and they, together with the landlord, Denis O'Donovan, ran out to surrender. The Auxiliaries continued to fire, wounding one of the RIC and killing O'Donovan, who was hit by six bullets. Capt. Wood then ordered fire to cease.

That, at least, was the official story. But the incident was witnessed by an eminent surgeon named Cripps, whose brother, Lord Parmoor, and nephew, Stafford Cripps, were in turn members of British Labour administrations. Cripps reported that the Auxiliaries rampaged around the hotel "like demented Red Indians". And his account was supported by members of the hotel staff who said that O'Donovan had been put up against a wall and shot. A week later, Lord Parmoor presented the evidence and a dum-dum cartridge to the House of Lords. An official enquiry produced the predictable whitewash, but the event helped to convince the military authorities that Auxiliaries should no longer be used as part of a police force.

His family history pushed O'Malley inevitably in the direction of Fianna Fáil. It was not even that his grandfather had been shot by the British or that, like many others, he admired South's courage and dedication. With a father and two uncles so deeply and so publicly involved, he must necessarily be of the party if not in it. Following in the family's footsteps was taken for granted in political as in professional matters; you were born into Fianna Fáil and that was that.

But when he eventually joined, as a student in University College, Dublin, he was too much an O'Malley to be a conventional member. At meetings in The Singing Kettle cafe in Leeson Street — the President of UCD, Michael Tierney, did not permit politicial organisations of any kind inside the college — he tended to debate issues in a sharp, intellectual style he had learned partly from the Jesuits in the Crescent and partly from regular reading of the *New Statesman,* the English socialist weekly edited by Kingsley Martin whose radical approach to politics he greatly admired. Contemporaries remember him as someone who could be highly entertaining, witty and provocative when he was with friends but suspicious and taciturn to the point of sullenness if outsiders joined the company. His adoption of the *New Statesman* and a fondness for the works of the French philosopher, Jacques Maritain, led him to conclusions that were, to say the least, unorthodox; and he was dismissive of less well-formed or less adventurous opinions, to which he was apt to reply with snorts of sarcasm.

At University Hall, the Jesuit residence where he stayed, he became auditor of the Debating Society and made a name for himself by insisting that Owen Sheehy-Skeffington, lately elected to the Senate for Trinity and, with Noel Browne and Jack McQuillan, considered an ogre of secular radicalism by the clerical establishment, should address the society. The Jesuits dug their heels in and refused permission. O'Malley persisted and Sheehy-Skeffington drew public attention to the affair in letters to the editor of *The Irish Times*. The Jesuits won in the end and O'Malley was left to run a debate with a former Taoiseach, John A. Costello, among the speakers and a vacant seat to symbolise the enforced absence of the controversial senator. It was, O'Malley likes to think, one of the dying kicks of the old regime which governed the country with a clerical veto and a censor's fist.

To O'Malley the ban on Sheehy-Skeffington was "sickening and quite hypocritical," like the fuss about the books of O'Faolain, O'Connor and O'Brien:

When you think about the passions that were engendered defending that situation, it really makes you sceptical about the passions engendered in defending certain situations today and how laughable they are going to be in ten or twenty years time.

My view is that if something is inevitably going to happen, it is foolish for a society or for some people within a society to struggle vehemently against it. If change is going to take place, the proper approach to it is to channel it in the direction that will be most beneficial to the whole society, the most appropriate direction. The worst attitude to take to change is an absolute, blank refusal to accept it, with the result that, when it does happen as inevitably it must, it bursts over you with all kinds of unpleasant consequences that might otherwise be avoided.

Unfortunately, I don't think that we have mentally adapted to a situation where we take advantage of what is going to happen. There are still too many in Ireland who consciously and deliberately fight against the inevitable and I think Ireland in every sense, socially and economically, has lost out by that.

He makes no great claims for the nights of debate in The Singing Kettle or University Hall, since they were never brought to bear on the old, inherited politics:

> We were engaged in an intellectual exercise; the real politics on the ground were quite different. When you think of it, there must have been a fair dose of hypocrisy about that too. You carried on an intellectual political life separate from your actual political life.

He was soon to be thrust, with brutal suddenness, into the real politics on the ground.

In at the Deep End

NEIL BLANEY WAS to suggest that Des O'Malley was not the candidate he would have chosen to replace his uncle, Donogh. It may well be Blaney's view in retrospect; at the time he worked so hard for O'Malley's election that he might have cost the party the seat.

Donogh O'Malley, who was among the brightest and best of Lemass's young Ministers, suffered a heart attack on the road between Sixmilebridge and Newmarket-on-Fergus in Co. Clare on a cold Sunday morning in the spring of 1968. He died almost immediately, leaving a legacy of highly coloured stories (many of them his own) about how he'd poked his finger in authority's jaundiced eye and made a very solid contribution towards the introduction of free secondary education.

His death also left Fianna Fáil with a by-election it had to win if its reputation were not to be severely damaged: Lemass had resigned two years earlier and had been replaced by Jack Lynch whom many still regarded as a caretaker Taoiseach, chosen to avoid the split that might have occurred had there been an open contest between Charlie Haughey and George Colley. As it was, the factions that were later to develop around Haughey and Colley were beginning to take shape; and the party's external critics were making much of its fund-raising organisation, Taca, which combined high living and patriotic rhetoric in a way that shocked its older members and more conservative supporters.

The party was vulnerable. The mood in the country favoured Labour — these were the years of concern about housing, of protest against speculation in building land and agitation for the public ownership of fisheries. The Labour Party in Limerick had chosen Mick Lipper, a popular but moderate man who could be guaranteed to take a chunk of the traditional O'Malley vote. Fine Gael had a young and enthusiastic solicitor called Jim O'Higgins whose party lineage was impeccable. Fianna Fáil needed an O'Malley. Des, who had qualified as a solicitor in 1962 and had taken over his father's practice in 1965, was the obvious choice. He was now 29, married to a highly articulate and independent-minded friend of his college days, Pat McAleer of Omagh, and the father of three children. But family protocol had to be observed and later some complications to be overcome, as he explained to Fintan O'Toole in an interview published in *Magill* in January 1986:

A couple of weeks after Donogh died quite a number

of them came to me and asked would I be interested and I said I wouldn't if Hilda, Donogh's widow, was interested (in standing). So I went to see her with a number of others and she expressed absolutely no interest whatever and, in fact, advised me strongly against it, told me that if I went into politics I'd have a miserable time and assured us all that she had no interest.

About twelve months or so later there was a General Election and I stood at that. By that time, she had changed her mind and told me that she wanted to stand and she wanted me to stand down. I thought about it, because I had to a large extent removed myself from the legal scene into the political scene, and I thought that I had something to offer. After discussing it with a lot of people including senior people within the government and Fianna Fáil, I decided that I would continue to stand and I did.

Among those who'd approached him in the first instance were Haughey, who'd been a close friend of his uncle, and Blaney, whose reputation as a winner of by-elections made him the toast of Fianna Fáil and the terror of its opponents. It was a bitterly fought election, though the bitterness was more evident among their supporters than between the candidates. Three days before polling, some of Blaney's more experienced electioneering friends arrived from Donegal and, somehow or other, the figure "77" appeared in red paint at street corners under O'Higgins's name. The meaning was clear: the red symbolised the blood of the 77 Republicans killed during the Civil War. O'Higgins's supporters certainly knew what it meant and at the count the Fine Gael candidate ironically thanked Blaney for his "splendid efforts in putting 77 under my name."

The Fianna Fáil vote had been cut by almost 2,500 and Lipper was ahead of O'Higgins on the first count, which meant that O'Malley had to depend on O'Higgins's transfers to be elected. He made it, but only just. In May 1986 in an RTE film marking the 60th anniversary of Fianna Fáil, Blaney remarked that he'd always found O'Malley "an irritable little man," suggesting that he'd never approved of him. Maybe he didn't; he could certainly find no reason for approving of him after the arms crisis of 1970 when Blaney and Haughey were sacked, their ally, Kevin Boland, resigned and O'Malley was promoted to the Department of Justice — "the irritable little man" had set himself squarely on the side of Lynch and Colley.

O'Malley, who had become Parliamentary Secretary to the Taoiseach after the 1969 election, had also declared himself unequivocally opposed to violence. In the controversy that swept Limerick after shots were fired at a Maoist bookshop in Castle Street in March, 1970, he was the most outspoken of local representatives, condemning an occurrence for which he held the city's ebullient mayor, Steve Coughlan, at least partly responsible. Coughlan, he said, had "tended to encourage violence from people who have been misled into thinking that shooting at Communists will help Christianity and democracy. The best way to safeguard Christianity and democracy is to practise it."

As for physical violence, using it "against those with whom we disagree" would "reduce ourselves to the level of Paisley and the B Specials." Shooting and bombing would replace one form of tyranny with another, equally obnoxious tyranny. But he advised keeping young people away from the Maoists.

This note of paternalism, bordering on cultural defence, was to be sounded again and again in his speeches and interviews during the early Seventies. Advocating EEC membership, for example, he argued that for far too long we had been cut off from the mainspring of European culture and dominated by the Anglo-American approach to life. We'd been culturally confined to a group consisting of Britain, Ireland, the United States and, to a lesser extent, Canada. And the most obtrusive example of our membership of "that unfortunate group" had been television: young people in Kerry were more familiar with certain English and American television personalities than with the members of the Kerry football team.

If the young were to be protected from the obtrusive effects of television, they were in even greater need of protection from the manipulation of extra-parliamentary agitators. In an interview with Maeve Binchy in *The Irish Times*, O'Malley said:

> I would not condemn the motivation and idealism of young — or indeed any — people who really thought that they were acting for valid reasons. But in a democracy these people must be prepared to accept as a result of their actions the full rigours of the law. What really does disturb me is the fact that so many serious and idealistic young people allow themselves to be used by professional agitators. You see the same people urging on almost any type of protest, and this negates idealism on their part.

And in the same interview:

> Communism is a danger because it does not direct its doctrines at the mature ... but at the young. Young, restless, immature people looking for change, for excitement, for something new. It is fundamentally wrong to encourage young people to defy authority in this way for motives that they barely understand. If you ask me am I against Communism, I tell you I am.

That was the spirit of the Forcible Entry Act, devised to deal with student occupations of Government Departments, the housing and fishery agitations of Sinn Féin and the unofficial protectors of Georgian buildings. It was, in a sense, the spirit of Fianna Fáil since it had lost the radicalism of the thirties. O'Malley was doing no more than following the party line.

But it was on 5 May 1970 that he arrived at the themes that were to dominate his political life for almost three years: loyalty to the Lynch/Colley faction in the party, the defeat of subversion and the defence of the institutions of the State. He was 31 and just two years in the Dáil when he became Minister for Justice. His appointment in place of Micheál O'Moráin, a survivor of Dev's last Cabinet, was the first public acknowledgment — the tip of the iceberg, as the Fine Gael leader, Liam Cosgrave, called it — that things had gone drastically wrong in the party and the Government.

The events that followed I have described in detail elsewhere.* After their dismissal, Blaney and Haughey, with John Kelly, a militant Belfast Republican, Jim Kelly, lately resigned from the Army and Albert Luykx, a businessman who was friendly with several Ministers, were accused of conspiring to import arms illegally. A District Justice found that Blaney had no case to answer; a jury in the High Court acquitted Haughey, Luykx and the Kellys. An investigation later by the Dáil's Committee of Public Accounts revealed that £76,000 from a £100,000 fund voted for the relief of distress in the North was missing.

The crisis had three sources. The first lay in the rhetorical anti-partitionism of Southern Nationalists, to which Fianna Fáil was particularly addicted. The second was the development since the leadership struggle in 1966 of factions inside the party which gave their allegiance to Colley, Haughey or the Boland-Blaney axis. The third, and the immediate

*The Party — Inside Fianna Fáil by Dick Walsh (Gill & MacMillan, Dublin 1986)

**Jack Lynch, leader of
Fianna Fáil 1966-79**
Derek Spiers/Report

**Peter Berry, Secretary
of the Department
of Justice**

Irish Press

Des O'Malley, Minister of Justice, receiving his Seal of Office, May 1970
Irish Press

cause of the crisis, was the outbreak of hostilities in the North in August 1969, an event which confronted the rhetoric with deadly reality and presented the factions with an issue on which to focus their attention.

O'Malley, as Parliamentary Secretary to the Taoiseach and the party's Chief Whip, was in a position to observe at uncomfortably close range the struggle which racked the Cabinet that August. Catholic areas in Belfast and Derry had come under attack from a combination of the RUC, B Specials and Loyalist forces. Blaney and Boland, who had long demanded a more militant response from the South, believed the attack presented an opportunity for direct intervention; Haughey, to the surprise of his colleagues, joined them, at least in the argument that a Border crossing by the Irish Army would cause the United Nations to intervene, thus providing the conflict with an international dimension.

O'Malley, who could only be a mute spectator in the Cabinet room, was never in any doubt where his loyalty lay. On his arrival in the Dáil, he had been expected to follow Donogh's lead and join Haughey's group. (Donogh had been Haughey's campaign manager in '66.) Instead, he chose to follow Lynch who, in his view, was continuing to implement the policies that Lemass had initiated, especially on the North. His admiration for the party leader grew as he watched him, first in isolation, then with the support of Colley and Paddy Hillery, who was Minister for External Affairs, take on the widely-feared strong men in an effort to preserve the Government, the party and the State.

He says of Haughey at this time:

It was not clear at first that he was taking an anti-Lynch line. He was certainly not, by any means, the most vocal of the Ministers and it seemed reasonable that, as he was in Finance, he should be on any committee [the cabinet sub-committee on which Haughey served with Blaney and Jim Gibbons, the Minister for Defence] that might have to take decisions at short notice, decisions which might have financial implications. When I discovered that he was involved in this other business, only a couple of days before my appointment to Justice, I was simply amazed.

"This other business" was what led to the charge of conspiring to import arms illegally and, as speaker after speaker told the Dáil during the debate that followed his and Blaney's dismissal, Haughey's alleged involvement amazed not only O'Malley but virtually everyone else.

O'Malley had two meetings with Haughey between his dismissal and the trials (one was abortive; the second ended with his acquittal). The first meeting, on a racecourse, lasted about a minute and a half: Haughey simply asked if he could see the new Minister, who said yes. The subject of the second meeting, which took place in an office in Leinster House, has not been disclosed, though Peter Berry, then Secretary of the Department of Justice, believed it had to do with his giving evidence at the trial. Shortly after the founding of the Progressive Democrats, Boland, Jim Kelly and others were to assert that it reflected badly on O'Malley that, as Minister for Justice, he should have met a man who was about to stand trial. O'Malley replied: "If these matters required explanation from anybody, it wasn't from me." To which he later added, in one of a series of interviews with this writer:

It's a matter of opinion [whether it was right or wrong to have met Haughey]. I suppose, in retrospect, I would not have met him, but it's easy to say that many years after the event. I am sure more serious errors of judgment have been made, both by me and by others, than that particular one.

To describe his two years and ten months in Justice as

difficult would be a feeble attempt to characterise a period which encompassed the aftermath of the arms crisis: widespread activity by para-militaries and their supporters, North and South; the introduction of internment in the North and a threat to introduce it in the Republic; the strengthening of the Offences Against the State Act and the establishment of the Special Criminal Court. It included Bloody Sunday, when 14 unarmed men were shot dead by Paratroopers in Derry, and along with internment such monumental blunders by British political leaders as their flirtation, as James Downey called it in *Them and Us*, with the Provisional IRA. 1972 was the North's most violent year, starting with Bloody Sunday and ending with a toll of 474 dead and thousands injured.

Nationalist passions were roused in the South as fear and hostility grew in both Nationalist and Loyalist camps in the North. Yet the British Government, which was deeply suspicious of all Irish politicians, and Fianna Fáil in particular, had to be convinced that the best hope for Anglo-Irish relations lay in putting an end to devolved government which guaranteed permanent Unionist rule from Stormont and attempting a political solution which would give both sides of the community a share in power. Dublin's interest in what happened in the North had to be acknowledged, Dublin's goodwill in the search for a settlement accepted. Lynch and his colleagues had to work hard and patiently to make themselves understood at home, in the North and in London. And if it meant taking harsh and unpopular actions in their own jurisdiction, there was more than popularity at stake: the Republican para-militaries, Official, Provisional and Saor Eire, had declared themselves the enemies of the Southern State as well as the North and Britain.

As for Fianna Fáil, O'Malley now recalls that its rhetoric was:

fairly far removed from reality when you had to meet it on the ground. It was easy to indulge in rhetoric when there was not an awful lot happening, but when human life began to be put in danger and human life began to be lost on a fairly wide scale, at any rate by Irish standards, you had to be very careful about the rhetoric and what you did. You could not indulge in fairly free and careless flag-waving. It became clear to a lot of us that you couldn't take the rhetoric literally, that here we were facing a very serious situation in which a lot of lives were at risk and a certain number of lives were lost. Our duty was to minimise, not to exacerbate, the risk and losses.

So he reacted to the intimidation of juries by introducing the non-jury Special Courts and to the threat to the State by amending the Offences Against the State Act. The flow of American funds to the IRA worried him, so he went to the United States to make one of the first appeals to Irish-Americans to stop sending money or weapons or both. On each occasion he argued that 95 per cent of the people were behind him and the Government. But, though he said he was determined to maintain an unarmed police force, that capital punishment should be used only as a last resort and though he set his face against widescale internment, he bluntly announced his intention of doing whatever proved necessary to defend the State and its institutions. Criticism came, not from within Fianna Fáil, but from journalists and civil liberties organisations; and he viewed both with considerable suspicion.

His inexperience, he now agrees, may have contributed to tougher action and sharper reactions than might otherwise have been the case:

Being conscious of your own shortcomings, due to lack of experience, made you sharper; but another factor which had a bearing during the first eight months or so was the Secretary who was then in the Department. [This was Peter Berry.] If you had had a more conventional Secretary, you could have been a little more relaxed about things and, perhaps, some of those things that arose you could take more readily in your stride. But Mr Berry was not a conventional Secretary and I had no experience of conventional Secretaries or how they operated at that time. Mr Berry would have been admirable for someone who had considerable experience, but he wasn't necessarily admirable for someone who had none.

Berry, who liked to be known as the grey eminence of the Department, considered himself an expert on subversion of all sorts but was particularly suspicious of movements on the Left. He cast a cold eye on the 11 Ministers he served and had differences with several of them, including Haughey and Brian Lenihan; he was to retire early, after which he unsuccessfully took actions for libel (against *The Irish Times*) and for compensation which he claimed Lynch and O'Malley had promised him. It had often been said that there was an air of paranoia in the Department at this time. O'Malley takes the point: "There were elements of it, certainly. The Department was a bit introspective. All Departments tend to look with suspicion on outsiders, but that was particularly so in Justice where a lot of the people felt a bit beleaguered and where they felt they were a bit cut off and were not fully understood."

It seems O'Malley, to some extent, shared the feeling:

You couldn't but be uncomfortable. Everything that was happening was happening for the first time and was, therefore, harder to cope with than if it had happened before. Another factor which made me feel uncomfortable and would have made anyone feel uncomfortable, if they were in that position and determined to handle things as I did, was the fact that you had fairly limited public sympathy and support, compared with the support that Ministers for Justice have subsequently had and you had very limited media support and pretty constant media criticism. Nowadays, Ministers for Justice tend to be criticised for not going far enough, not taking strict enough steps, not making even more fundamental changes in the law against criminal or subversive elements. It was quite otherwise at that time. It was very early on in the North's troubles and a lot of things that subsequently became clear to the public were not clear to the public then.

Yes, I did feel misunderstood. I still feel it. It was 16 years ago and the traditional, Republican, romantic ideas were fresher in people's minds than they are now. There was a generation of people who were less far removed from the War of Independence than people are today and when they thought about the modern IRA, so-called, they tended to think about people like Sean South and O'Hanlon; a lot of reasonable people were not entirely unsympathetic at that time. The same kind of people now, either the same people or the same kind of people, would be utterly unsympathetic because they now see that these are not the same as [the men of] 1916 or 1921, nor are they the Sean Souths or the O'Hanlons. They see them as a dangerous element whose idealism is negligible.

Was the change inevitable?

Events in Northern Ireland caused some of the shift. I think there were different people involved in the beginning, some basically decent people, but they got pushed aside and the thing became more and more vicious, more and more ruthless, more and more unChristian as it went along. But people who might more readily be rejected were able

The Minister for Justice presenting the Commemorative Garda Medal to Deputy Commissioner Ned Garvey, 21 December 1972

Irish Times

The Fianna Fáil Cabinet, 1977

Irish Press

to buy time for themselves with the ham-fisted approach of the British with internment and Bloody Sunday.

His criticism of internment in the North has been voiced again and again, yet he had threatened to introduce internment in the South at the end of 1970. He explains:

What they did was on an enormously wide scale with hundreds and hundreds of people involved. What we had in mind was to pose the threat that if we were forced to do this we would do it, in relation to a small number of people, in order to prevent a certain event happening which would have been enormously damaging from this country's point of view. It's one thing to threaten that; it's another actually to intern many hundreds of people, a lot of them on very thin grounds.

He will not say what the potentially damaging event was:

All that is proper for me to say is that information was passed on to us by the Gardai. It wasn't my job to inquire where they got it. It's not the Minister's, or for that matter the Department's job. But you have to talk to them to assess the weight they place on the information they have received. In that particular instance, they seemed to regard it as quite reliable and the suggestion was that we would be very well advised to act on it in order to forestall a certain type of thing happening.

As to the rumour that it was a kidnap or death threat to Berry, he says: "It had nothing to do with Peter Berry, nothing."

In the *Magill* interview he told Fintan O'Toole that the kind of event the Gardai feared — and worse — had happened afterwards. If not Berry, the target is most likely to have been an industrialist or a diplomat. And assuming that the threat came from Saor Eire, the counter-threat of internment was made effective by leaning on the IRA:

What we decided to do (was) to threaten to do it and convey to a much more sizeable subversive organisation the fact that we were considering that and let them exert pressure to see that this matter didn't happen. It wouldn't have suited the more sizeable organisation. And that's the way it worked.

Tough talking worked in the party, certainly as far as those delegates who attended the 1972 Ard-Fheis were concerned. John Healy, never one of O'Malley's admirers, described it in *The Irish Times* as The Year of the Cheering Doves. Healy wrote:

The highlight of yesterday was Dessie O'Malley's speech, laying it on the line... it was fearless speaking and he had read the mood of the Ard-Fheis. He was cheered when he called for an end to ambivalence and when he had finished there was a move made to give him a standing ovation. He may not be the most popular young Minister and the most likeable personality, but the Ard-Fheis admired his guts and their instinct was right.

Perhaps of even greater significance was Healy's comment that, on this issue, "the people of Ireland were ahead of their elected leaders."

37

Back to the Green Line

O'MALLEY LEFT THE Department of Justice with considerable relief, though the image that had been imprinted on many minds was to survive for years. He was easily caricatured as spiky, impatient and uncompromising. Journalists remembered the sting of his reference to the mosquito press long after they had forgotten the context in which it was made: an attempt to prohibit incitement in the Forcible Entry Bill, a measure which, as he forecast, was to fade from the public memory more quickly than it passed through the Oireachtas.

Several years later, all hell was to break over Liam

39

Cosgrave's head when he declared that violence was killing the desire for unity. By then, of course, Cosgrave as Taoiseach, Pat Cooney in Justice and Conor Cruise O'Brien, as Labour's spokesman on the North (he was also Minister for Posts & Telegraphs) had replaced Lynch, Colley and O'Malley in the demonology of Nationalists and Fianna Fáil had plunged again into the greenery to which the party invariably retreats when it finds itself in opposition.

Cosgrave's observation was no more than a statement of fact. It was, moreover, a fact recognised in every action taken by Lynch and O'Malley in support of their attitudes to the North and domestic security between 1970 and 1973; and there was nothing in the recognition which was inconsistent with the approach to unity adopted by either de Valera or Lemass. As Ronan Fanning wrote in his epilogue to the volume *Independent Ireland:*

> What is remarkable is not how much but how little the high drama of events in Northern Ireland since 1968 have impinged upon politics and society in the Republic, despite occasional exceptions such as the referendum of December 1972 deleting the clause in the 1937 Constitution which accorded a ''special position'' to the Catholic Church ... In most respects life in the South seemed far removed from what most citizens in the Republic saw less as their problem than as the ''Northern Troubles''. Indeed, Southern self-interest and apprehension consequent on the vision of long years of bloody carnage on their television screens may well have further reinforced the partitionist mentalities of a people few of whom would contemplate venturing north of the Border. Sixty years of freedom would seem rather to have persuaded many in independent Ireland to take secret consolation from the reflection which their Head of State, Eamon de Valera, voiced publicly in

1963: "Ireland is Ireland without the North."

De Valera, in conversations with O'Malley, endorsed the action taken by Lynch to secure the future of the party, the Government and the State. The conversations took place in Árus an Uachtaráin where the Minister accompanied judges when they received their seals of office from the President. O'Malley was to report:

> He left me in no doubt at all that he was entirely in agreement with and supportive of Jack Lynch. This applied both to his Northern policy generally and to the actions he had taken within the party.

Some commentators seemed dubious of the endorsement, though John Bowman's thoroughly researched and scrupulously documented account of *De Valera and The Ulster Question* leaves no room for doubt: Dev had long ago come to accept the gradualist approach, publicly admitting that the achievement of unity would be a long haul.

Cosgrave and Garret FitzGerald, his Minister for Foreign Affairs, followed the Lynch line. With the British Government, moderate Unionists, the SDLP and Alliance, they negotiated the Sunningdale Agreement, establishing for the first time a Northern administration in which Unionists and non-Unionists shared power. It was to last less than six months, but it was a brave attempt to escape the sectarian fetters of traditional politics and it was, as John Hume acknowledged at Sunningdale, a logical conclusion to the discussions with Britain that Jack Lynch had initiated. But Lynch, tactically outflanked by Blaney, who had now been expelled from the party, was forced to oppose the Agreement in the Dáil.

It was the old story. What might have been perfectly acceptable, indeed an admirable and progressive step towards a resolution of the Northern problem, if it had been brought

41

to a conclusion by Fianna Fáil, must of necessity be suspect in the hands of a Coalition government. Lemass, in similar circumstances, had objected to the establishment of the Industrial Development Authority and the encouragement of foreign investment, though he had already proposed both and was to be more closely identified than anyone else with the implementation of the proposals. No one was shocked or even surprised by this: since Fianna Fáil was the only party fit to run the country, it was virtually a law of nature. O'Malley didn't quite swallow the law hook, line and sinker, but it caused him to make one of those statements which have since been quoted to prove — unnecessarily, since like Lemass he makes no bones about it — that he changed his mind.

Shortly after Sunningdale, he said:

> At last a situation exists in the North in which every section of the community has a say in the government of the Six Counties. No longer is the minority there totally and permanently excluded from sharing in power.

> One can hopefully come to the conclusion, therefore, that the blatant injustices and discrimination that were the hallmark of Unionist rule for half a century are coming to an end. For these reasons, any reasonable Irishman must welcome the principles of this Agreement. In general, it embodies the objectives which the Fianna Fáil Government strove for, for several years, up to 1973. Without the groundwork and without the patient tenacity of Jack Lynch, Paddy Hillery and others, the British Government and a large segment of the Unionist party would never have accepted the concept of power-sharing in the way they do now.

So far so good. Then came the objections — to ''some of the typographical trick-o'-the-loopery'' — and the doubts about the Coalition's commitment to the national aspiration:

> The glibness with which some of them talk of a new Constitution makes many people suspicious that such a move would only be a device to achieve a situation where the rights of the whole Irish people to determine their destiny together is swept away.

> If our right to unity, which follows from the desire of a majority of the Irish people for unity, is taken away, there can be no long-term solution of our problems. Ireland is one Ireland, one nation, one country because God made it one. That essential unity cannot be put asunder by the anti-national semantics of Conor Cruise O'Brien or Garret FitzGerald.

There is no account of how his audience, at a meeting of the Fianna Fáil Comhairle Dáil Ceantair in Virginia, Co. Cavan, reacted to this speech — probably with cheers of "Up the Republic!"

O'Malley was, clearly and quite consciously, having it both ways, giving the Agreement the chance that any reasonable Irishman would demand but doubting the ability or will of the Coalition to see it through in the proper national spirit. Re-dedicating himself, the party and the people to the national aspiration — "because God made it one" — he was also pre-empting trouble at a potentially difficult Ard Fheis.

Two years later, speaking in Limerick, his criticism of the Coalition was a good deal more extreme and much more extravagantly expressed:

> Men of violence are doing far less harm to Ireland than the outspoken people now in government who are progressively destroying the economic and democratic fabric of our society.

Dismissing their warnings of imminent civil war in the North as an attempt to divert attention from the fact that the Republic was facing economic breakdown, he continued:

The resultant chaos, which will arise when public servants and social welfare recipients can no longer be paid, will allow great freedom of action to anarchists and extremists of all kinds to overthrow our institutions and establish some form of totalitarian regime in Ireland.

Some of his critics have suggested that by now, January 1976, he was simply reacting to Haughey's return to the front bench in the autumn of the previous year. If the implication is that he saw himself in competition with Haughey for Nationalist support, this is not so. In the passage just quoted there are both echoes of his days in Justice — the old paranoia — and some foreshadowing of the future — fear of economic breakdown. Here, and in a speech about how the North as an entity had failed, he was reflecting a growing conviction that social and economic chaos represented a major threat to democracy, North and South. It was a threat that he believed was being ignored as attention focussed on Nationalism in its para-military and political forms or on Unionism bent on maintaining the Union at any price. Both "isms", he believed, were destined to lead to self-destruction.

His views about contraception and public morality generally, as expressed in a contribution to the 1974 controversy, were less soundly based and, in retrospect, are easily ridiculed. It was a controversy that produced few creditable performances; its main ingredients were legal confusion, moral hypocrisy and political farce — and no one got what they wanted. The Control of Importation, Sale and Manufacture of Contraceptives Bill was intended to do what its title suggested. Because of a Supreme Court decision in the McGee case in 1973, contraceptives were being freely and legally imported. They could not be sold, though they could be given away; but it would only be a matter of time, Pat

Cooney believed, before an attempt to legalise their sale succeeded. The Bill's main provision was to legalise the sale through licensed outlets, but to married couples only. It might be unenforceable, but so what? — so, to some degree at least, were a lot of other measures. It was, of course, a Government Bill? Well, it was and it wasn't. Cooney, its author, was the Minister for Justice, but to accommodate conscientious objectors there was to be a free vote on the Government side. Fianna Fáil had no such let-out. The party had both moral and practical objections to the Bill and would not allow its members to follow their consciences if, indeed, any of them felt conscientiously bidden to support it.

Looking back on the debate, from a distance of twelve years, it is as if most of the participants were merely rehearsing their arguments for the second debate on contraception or the debates on abortion and divorce. Those who supported change called attention to the changing needs of the electorate; they underlined the primacy of the Oireachtas and the wisdom and justice of separating the functions of Church and State, and they pointed to the contradictions between talk of unity and partitionist practices. The bishops had said it was the legislators' duty to legislate; would the legislators not take them at their word? They wouldn't.

The opponents of change stuck to their guns. Oliver J. Flanagan summed up the views of most of them:

As sure as this Bill goes on the Statute Books it will be the raising of the sluice gates of every kind of immorality with the ultimate result of abortion and all that abortion stands for.

Here they are, a Fianna Fáil man commented:

bringing in a Contraception Bill that will ruin the quality of life to which Irish people were used throughout the

45

centuries and for which generations fought and died — and there was no talk of contraception... If you bring in a Bill to make murder legal you won't get me to vote for it.

O'Malley poured scorn on the side-effects of licensing 1,500 or 2,000 outlets — ordinary shops, where chemists were not available — for the sale of contraceptives:

It will make a splendid addition to the often charming notepaper of traders in the west to read that, as well as being licensed for all other things for which it is possible to be licensed, they can also proudly boast that they are licensed under Subsection (3) of Section 2 of the Control of Importation, Sale and Manufacture of Contraceptives Act. I doubt if they will fit it all into one line.

He had one or two practical suggestions — for example, that clinics might supply contraceptives to people who were advised by their doctors that they needed them, or that importation for personal use might be permitted. In fact, when he was a Minister he had had a note on this very subject from a Cabinet colleague (presumed to be Erskine Childers). The note, which Cooney read to the Dáil, provoked a certain amount of hilarity:

If, therefore, it is decided that the use of condoms cannot be proscribed, there seems to be no alternative to allowing importation in limited quantities for personal use either in personal luggage or through the post. This raises a question of what is a limited quantity. Twenty at any one time might be a reasonable compromise.

But, people wanted to know, for how long might this limited quantity be judged sufficient? A week, a month, or a year? No one seemed sure.

It was, however, on the duty of a legislator that O'Malley made his most controversial comment. In the Supreme Court, one of the judges had said that in his view, in any ordered society, the protection of morals through the deterrence of fornication and promiscuity was a legitimate legislative aim and a matter not of private but of public morality.

"I respectfully agree," said O'Malley.

Our duty as a legislature is, so far as we can within the confines of our Constitution, as interpreted for us by the Supreme Court, to deter fornication and promiscuity, to promote public morality and to prevent, insofar as we can — there are, of course, clear limitations on the practicability of that — public immorality.

Ten and a half years later, on the same subject, indeed on the amendment of the legislation which was eventually passed, in 1979, he made his speech which ended with the words: "I stand by the Republic."

In 1974 the contraception issue left no one covered in glory: Cosgrave, accompanied by his Minister for Education, Dick Burke, and five Fine Gael backbenchers — Tom Enright, Martin Finn, Des Governey, Joe McLaughlin and Oliver J. Flanagan — crossed the floor to vote with the Opposition. The Bill was defeated by 61 votes to 75. John Kelly, the Government's Chief Whip, trying to put a brave face on it, made matters worse by claiming that because five-sixths of the Coalition's deputies had voted for the measure it was a memorable occasion: "If we are ever to have an all-Ireland day of national brotherhood this would be no bad date to choose."

But if 16 July 1974 gets into the history books it will be because it was the day on which a Prime Minister helped to defeat his Government's Bill.

No one got what they wanted. Those who sought to keep the floodgates tightly shut left them open; as a result of their efforts, condoms could be imported by the millions — and they were. Those who were hoping for a modest, even restrictive reform — because they knew the others would object if they asked for more — found themselves inundated. O'Malley would obviously prefer that his contribution should remain a footnote to the inglorious affair.

The Road to Damascus

TO POLITICIANS OF the traditional school, all converts are suspect. For one thing, converts tend to prove their new loyalties by being more zealous than the rest; and zealots are a threat to those who, more than anything else, value quiet lives. You do not have to be a cynic to observe that in Irish politics changing your mind is only slightly less disturbing than demonstrating that you have a mind to change.

When O'Malley was expelled from Fianna Fáil, Michael D. Higgins of the Labour Party made the comment:

He was accused of having ideas. To be an intellectual,

even of the Right, is a very much greater disability in Irish politics than being sexually perverse.

And when he set up the Progressive Democrats, his former colleagues took the traditional view: Brian Lenihan, the Deputy Leader of Fianna Fáil, dismissed it as a flash in the pan, to which Haughey, remembering months later one of Micheal O'Moráin's bucolic sayings, added that if a hen left her nest to lay out once she was likely to do it again.

Traditionalists are convinced that all conversions occur with the suddenness of that famous fall on the road to Damascus; and as far as they are concerned, Saul might as well have kept his own name and stayed on his horse. To them, O'Malley's new outlook was no more than a Pauline revelation inspired, not by a fall from a horse but by personal animosity towards the horseman Haughey. The simple explanation was: pique.

Of the personal animosity there was never any doubt. In the factional divisions of 20 years, personal allegiance was as potent an influence as political conviction; and style as much as any claim to continuity showed where you stood. If Haughey's people saw the supporters of Lynch, Colley and O'Malley as thin-skinned and media-conscious Free Staters, their opponents looked on Haughey's people as yahoos, a description applied by one of Cork's old-timers to both their personal and political behaviour.

In some ways, the personalities of the leaders are so different as to make friendship difficult, in other ways they are so alike as to make it impossible. Both are temperamentally impetuous, impatient and uncompromising. Haughey, the self-made man, enjoys a lifestyle of conspicuous grandeur; O'Malley, with his comfortable background, dislikes ostentation and suspects it in others. Haughey favours adulation; O'Malley decries the cult of personality. The

Des O'Malley, prior to his challenge for the leadership of Fianna Fáil
Irish Times

Charlie Haughey, after the challenge had been withdrawn
Irish Times

Fianna Fáil leader looks down from on high over the crowds at his Ard-Fheiseanna; at the Progressive Democrats' conference, the leader's portrait was missing.

Haughey, a liberal of the mohair-suited Sixties, has grown conservative to the point where Fianna Fáil earns the title "The Bishops' Party." O'Malley, the conservative of the Seventies, has become liberal — at least on social issues. But when Haughey was forced to join the ranks of the financially orthodox in 1982, O'Malley was one of the persuaders, allowing the Workers' Party leader, Tomás Mac Giolla, to claim that — freed of his influence — Fianna Fáil would become again a high-spending party. Haughey, the populist, is content to let the claim stand; O'Malley, with a more limited constituency, remains wedded to orthodoxy.

Both have an eye for horses and a gambling instinct. Both enjoy the arts, though in different styles: O'Malley likes to take part in readings of *Ulysses*; Haughey prefers to be known as a patron, the Minister who introduced the popular tax concessions for artists and the inspiration of Aosdana. The patron suspects the artist of subversion; and the artist is convinced the patron wants to own him ...

But O'Malley's political differences with what was to become, under Haughey, the accepted Fianna Fáil line had begun to emerge well in advance of the leadership contest with Colley in 1979, making the trouble that followed that contest inevitable. Personal animosity was merely the stone on which the blades were sharpened.

Twice during 1976 O'Malley came up with suggestions that revealed a changing approach to social affairs. He proposed "a humane and compassionate law on annulment" to obviate the need for a potentially divisive referendum on divorce; and he called for integrated education, throughout the country but particularly in the North, as a means of making it feasible for people of all traditions to live together. In the course of preparations for the 1977 election, he favoured the strategy adopted in the manifesto which Haughey privately derided and, on arrival in leadership, publicly repudiated. O'Malley still believes that the strategy was correct and argues that the real mistake was in failing to change it when conditions took a turn for the worse at the end of the Seventies.

From the Opposition benches he took part, with Colley, in the long and bitter resistance to the Coalition's programme of capital taxation and, in a protracted debate with Justin Keating, he disputed the merits of Keating's deal with the mining company, Bula. As Minister for Industry and Commerce, after 1977, he was no less forthright and controversial. He favoured a new emphasis in industrial strategy to help small, Irish-based companies — and claimed a success. He took on the international oil companies — and lost. When Ferenka, a multi-national operating in his own constituency, offered to keep its plant going, but at the expense of the Irish taxpayers, he called the offer outrageous. Ferenka closed. He advocated nuclear power as the cleanest and most efficient way of meeting the country's energy needs in the following decade; and it was only after a year of sustained pressure that he agreed to hold a public enquiry into the use of nuclear power before quietly dropping altogether the idea of siting a plant at Carnsore Point in Co. Wexford.

All the while he was moving closer to the political and economic philosophy which was to inform the Progressive Democrats. In March 1979 he told Olivia O'Leary in an interview published in *The Irish Times:*

There's nothing wrong with the fact that there hasn't been the ideological divide in politics here that Britain has had.

If our two main parties had split on the national question, so, in a sense, had the two main parties in the United States — but the old Civil War issues didn't count there anymore.

In the same interview, he hinted at what would now come under the heading of rolling back the influence of the State. Describing Fianna Fáil as a party of economic pragmatism, he selected Posts and Telegraphs as an example of an area in which private enterprise might usefully be introduced into the public sector.

He said:

> Public enterprise in the Department of Posts and Telegraphs has fallen down. That will have to be changed. I would like to see private telecommunications expertise brought into it in some way. The answer may be a semi-State body with access to the technology and expertise of one of the major telephone companies in the world.

NET (Nitrigin Eireann Teoranta), a semi-State company that came within the ambit of his own responsibilities, provided another example where, in his view, public enterprise and attitudes to public spending had gone wrong. The company had "gone way over their time and budget" in the building of a major plant. There had been constant stoppages which would not have arisen with a private company: "The public attitude to the taxpayer's money is that it's fair game."

He now explains:

> I had begun to veer towards things that would work rather than things that seemed all right on paper but stood a considerable risk of not working in practice. I think I've followed those lines, become more convinced of those views, — it's more important, in economic and commercial matters, that you let the system work rather than that you

interfere with it constantly and try to fiddle around with it.

The best thing for a Government to do is, within reason, to stand back. A Government has to maintain control over competition and so on. Otherwise, you are going to have cartels growing up with price fixing and all sorts of activity of that kind which is damaging to the public interest. But I don't think you should have the State seeking to involve itself to any significant degree in things that other people can do better.

It was the thinking here for a very long time, when the protected industries were being established under Lemass, that the State did not become involved if there was something that private enterprise could do or even might do. They tended to confine themselves to things that were of a scale or of a nature that it was most unlikely that private interests would ever become involved. And there used to be a maxim within Departments like Industry and Commerce that the State would take care not to compete unfairly with people who were taking risks with their own money.

A lot of that has gone by the board and the State's involvement, inevitable to some extent because of the changed circumstances, has grown. The State has involved itself extremely widely and a lot of its involvement has been extremely unsuccessful from any point of view.

And by this route he arrived at the conclusion that it was now time to roll back its influence:

It's the mainstream of European economic thinking. We in Ireland, alone of West European countries, are not seeking for the State to divest itself of a lot of its assets. That's a common practice throughout Europe today — where there are assets that are not beneficially held by the State.

I can't see much point in the State's retaining things on which it gets no return, and it has lots of assets on which it gets no returns and many assets on which it gets a negative return, has to subsidise them by borrowing at 11 or 12 per cent.

That makes absolutely no sense and it's widely recognised that it makes no sense. The place where the new economic thinking is being practised most widely at the moment is in France. There the State had acquired over the years a huge conglomeration of different interests but is now rapidly divesting itself of those interests on behalf of the French Exchequer. Even though there is a Socialist President in power, the indications are that he is not going to use the powers that he has to block that development or to put any very serious difficulty in its way.

In Britain it's a bit different — and Britain is where most Irish people see this happening — because the way that it's being done, as so much that's done there nowadays, is rather antagonistic. It's being done in a sense that is almost ideological rather than practical. It's being done for the sake of doing it rather than because it's right and the antagonism that it has engendered in some quarters in Britain has tended to overspill here. If it were looked on as it is in continental Europe, the reaction would be quite different.

The thing to remember, too, is that it's in countries like France and Britain that this is happening, countries where consumption by the State of GNP is very substantially less than ours; and if they feel that it's an appropriate policy to divest themselves of a lot of those assets, then very clearly it's an appropriate policy for us to follow. Here, the State has become so involved that it's stifled the willingness of a lot of people to take any kind of risk.

The State has portrayed itself, particularly in the last ten years, though the seeds were there well before that, as the purveyor of virtually everything good and the preventor of everything bad. The State is seen in this country, nowadays, as the place of first resort rather than, as I would see it, the place of last resort. The State should be where you turn when all else has failed, not the very first thing that comes into your mind.

But did private enterprise work when, as in 1977, it was supposed to have been the engine of growth?

The strategy worked very well for a number of years. Confidence returned and employment increased. But it went seriously wrong from the middle of 1979 because of the totally changed economic scenario here and worldwide as a result of the Iranian revolution and all the things that flowed from it. Huge increases in the price of oil had a devastating effect on nearly all Western economies and particularly on ours. If that hadn't happened, the situation would have been different. But by the middle of '79, we had the lowest unemployment figures in the history of the State. Employment was there for almost everyone who seriously wanted it.

Of course there was some unemployment. We have here people who are classified as unemployed but who would be classified differently elsewhere. There are people who are paid an element of social support for perfectly valid reasons — for instance, to keep them on the land — but who are not unemployed in the sense that they are going out looking for a job. And at that time unemployment was almost negligible. So it wouldn't be correct to say that the strategy didn't work. It worked up to the time of the changed external circumstances. Insofar as there was a mistake, it was that the whole thrust of the thinking was not changed radically or reversed more rapidly. I think it took too long for the realisation of the changed circumstances to sink in and a great deal of damage was done by the time the engines were reversed.

Haughey was now leader and Taoiseach. Colley, in spite of reservations, decided to stay on after he had been given a say in the appointments to Justice and Defence. O'Malley was happy enough to remain in Industry and Commerce. He believed that Haughey was about to make the changes he considered necessary in the Government's economic and financial policies. The new Taoiseach had announced that the country was living beyond its means and promised stern remedies. O'Malley now admits:

I was very glad, very relieved to hear what he had to say because I was afraid that he wouldn't say it. Unfortunately, the policies that were pursued subsequently were not policies that flowed from that analysis. Not policies which would have coped with the problems that the analysis highlighted.

Colley's reservations were expressed in a speech in which he said that the campaign that had been mounted against Jack Lynch had changed the party's rule about loyalty to its leader. He would be loyal to Haughey as Taoiseach, but not as leader of Fianna Fáil. O'Malley, who made no comment at the time, confesses to seeing things in a somewhat different light and in doing so answers a point that has often been made about his own willingness to serve:

There is, certainly, a distinction between the Taoiseach and the leader of a party. But you can serve under a Taoiseach who might not be your choice — as leader and, therefore, as Taoiseach — and serve quite freely under him. That, perhaps, is what George Colley had in mind, but he expressed it in a way that suggested he was practically going out of his way to be disloyal. I think he was being a bit unfair to himself.

Someone working in his Cabinet does not have to agree with the Taoiseach or support him in a personal sense. That distinction has been made before. And there are, no doubt, people in the present Cabinet who don't support Garret FitzGerald as leader of Fine Gael. It doesn't stop them working within the Cabinet. Of course, it's very much the case in other countries; the most obvious example of it is in various Thatcher Cabinets since 1979 when there were always several people who were not at all enamoured of Mrs Thatcher as leader of the party and Prime Minister, but who worked with her — and a lot of them did it very successfully.

But Haughey, with his presidential style, made changes:

Disagreement on policy was regarded as synonymous with personal disloyalty. A valid and genuine disagreement on policy was seen as some kind of personal attack, which it wasn't. And if you can't have disagreement on policy articulated within the Cabinet, then the form of Cabinet Government that we have becomes redundant. If you really want to have the presidential style of Government, the American type of Cabinet, much more closely reflecting the President's thinking, then you have a different system. It's arguable that some people might feel we should change our system but until we do we have this system and we would be better advised to work it as it was intended.

With the debate lost inside the Cabinet he took his case to a wider audience. Still a Minister — and prepared to serve again, until Haughey's demand for personal support became so insistent that he quit the Cabinet altogether in October 1982 — he attempted to initiate a discussion, both inside and outside the party, on the nature of Republicanism. In a major

Fianna Fáil Parliamentary Party meeting at which O'Malley withdrew as candidate for party leader, February 1982
Derek Spiers/Report

Receiving the Seal of Office as Minister for Industry and Commerce from President Hillery, and congratulations from Charlie Haughey, March 1982   Irish Press

speech delivered at a Fianna Fáil function in Scariff, Co. Clare in January 1981, he declared:

There is a certain disorientation in Irish society, not only about the shape of our future but also about our own aims and ideals. The old certainties have lost their force. We are just over the crest of a hill. We can look back to reassure ourselves of the distance we have travelled, but the path to the next line of hills is different and unfamiliar... I would like to use this opportunity to outline what, in my view, Fianna Fáil and indeed Republicanism in its true sense stands for today and in what our conception of Irish society now and in the future should consist.

This was what he had to say:

On State bodies —

Some have exhibited all the best characteristics of commercially oriented private enterprise; others have been abysmal failures. But no matter what the results have been, public bodies and authorities must not be allowed to engulf or stifle private enterprise and individual initiatives or to swallow up too large a share of national resources.

On self-reliance —

We must look primarily to ourselves, if we wish to catch up with the standard of living prevailing on the continent of Europe, one of the main tasks for the rest of the century. Regional funds and social funds are really no more than compensation for the effects of free trade. They do nothing to close the prosperity gap.

On the meaning of Republicanism —

There may be those among you who wonder what the realisation of our economic potential has to do with Republicanism. There is still a popular conception that Republicanism is a gun in one hand and a proclamation in the other and that its essence lies in an endless and self-

61

torturing preoccupation with the great national questions.

In my belief the prosperity, security, welfare and development, both spiritual and material, of the whole Irish people on a democratic and egalitarian basis, are the purposes for which the Republican ideal exists.

Haughey had said that the North had failed as a political entity. O'Malley, in this speech, added: "The North has also failed as an economic entity."

What he meant by failure —

The fleeting prosperity that came to flower in the Sixties, built over the foundations of discrimination, has collapsed; and the prospects, despite disproportionate aid from Britain, for restoring employment are grim for many years ahead... The abject dependence on large subsidies and on special pleading for favours from Westminster makes a mockery of a proud tradition of sturdy self-reliance.

On the old, authentic voice of Protestant Ireland, he quoted the Volunteers at Dungannon in 1782 —

We hold the right of private judgment in matters of religion to be equally sacred in others as in ourselves; as men and as Irishmen, as Christians and as Protestants, we rejoice in the relaxation of the penal laws against our Roman Catholic fellow subjects, and we conceive the measure to be fraught with the happiest consequences for the Union and the prosperity of the inhabitants of Ireland.

On the patriotism of Unionists —

None will deny that most Unionists love Ireland, or at least the part they know and live in, which they and their ancestors have helped to build up, and from which nobody is going to drive them. Our only wish is that their patriotism could be of benefit to us all.

On British withdrawal —

I doubt very much if today our biggest difficulty

regarding the North will be in trying peacefully to persuade the British eventually to leave. Rather will the really serious problems in the longer term be the reconciliation of the two traditions in the North and the creation of trust and co-operation between them.

On the Irish language —

In cherishing what is unique to us we do this because we recognise its importance, its value and its fragility; there is no implied hostility to other parts of our cultural heritage which are more self-supporting... Irish culture, while properly giving a special place to what is unique, is and must be recognised to be broadly based, comprehending all that Irish life and imagination has produced, regardless of the idiom in which it is expressed. This way we will discourage bald assertions that the ethos of our Republic is Gaelic, a half-truth which allows it to be misrepresented as alien to other traditions on this island. Davis referring to Ireland said that a national without a language of its own is only half a nation. Let us take care that the opposite is not also true, that having saved our language we do not remain half a nation.

On the nature of the State —

This is a democratic not a theocratic State; there are no Ayatollahs on this side of the Border ... Republicanism embraces and underlies our whole national development. It is the philosophy of this party. We have a duty to retain and develop it in our own hands, and not allow it to be misused and discredited. Republicanism in our sense reflects the true wishes and aspirations of the Irish people for freedom and independence, their confidence in the Irish nation and in a national life, their desire for progress and development, their demand for equal opportunity, for justice, toleration, order and reconciliation.

It was a challenge — and a provocative one — but it was directed at Fianna Fáil, not at its leader. In the event, it was not taken up by anyone. The response was: silence.

Standing by the Republic

O'MALLEY'S SPEECH IN Scariff failed to provoke a discussion in Fianna Fáil; and perhaps his most serious complaint about the party from then until his expulsion four years later was the absence of debate about where it stood and what it represented, as Ireland stumbled towards what he'd called at Scariff the next line of hills.

It wasn't that the period was uneventful. The years since Fianna Fáil's historic victory in 1977 have been crowded with happenings that demand to be set in the context of a coherent philosophy. None of the attempts to respond to that demand has come from Fianna Fáil; and none from any other source has fully captured the public mood or imagination.

There have been five changes of leadership in the three long-established parties since the '77 election. FitzGerald took over from Cosgrave while Fine Gael was still numbed by the size of its defeat; and Haughey outmanoeuvred Colley while Fianna Fáil still enjoyed its twenty-seat majority. There have been three challenges to Haughey, only one of which — the last, in early 1983 — came close to succeeding. In Labour, Brendan Corish was succeeded by Frank Cluskey and Cluskey, on losing his Dáil seat, by Michael O'Leary. O'Leary, after an internal defeat, jumped to Fine Gael and Labour turned in disbelief to Dick Spring.

There have been three elections, two of which, in June 1981 and February 1982, produced Governments that had to depend on the support of Independents and minorities — and fell when the props were withdrawn. But the electoral shifts were slight: those who had moved from Fine Gael to Fianna Fáil in '77 moved back in November '82; the Workers' Party acquired three and held two seats as Labour's popularity declined then recovered briefly; there was no great resurgence of Independents. At the time of writing, the PDs had yet to contest an election and Sinn Féin had only just decided to take Dáil seats, if it won any.

Not since the Fifties has the Republic suffered such severe and prolonged economic difficulties as those which began in mid '79 and not in this century has there been such a sustained increase in unemployment, unrelieved until the mid-Eighties by the safety valve of emigration. Membership of the European Monetary System has not prevented the development of the deepest financial crisis for decades.

The New Ireland Forum was set up to devise a Nationalist response to the continuing challenge of the Northern conflict. Fianna Fáil agreed reluctantly to join Fine Gael, Labour and the SDLP in the Forum but no sooner had it produced a report in May, 1984 than Haughey entered reservations about the options it presented. He was convinced that unity was not merely the first, it was the only choice.

After a disastrous start, when Margaret Thatcher rejected all options, negotiations with Britain on the basis of the report produced an Anglo-Irish Agreement giving the Republic for the first time a say in the affairs of the North, to which Unionists and Loyalists immediately took violent exception. Haughey had rejected it in advance and repeated his objections on its publication in November 1985.

The Fianna Fáil leader's refusal to hold internal discussions on the Forum report led to the first in his final series of disagreements with O'Malley. Haughey insisted that he alone had the right to speak publicly on the subject. O'Malley argued that since Ray MacSharry, one of Haughey's supporters, had been allowed to give an interview following the leader's line, he too should be permitted to present his views.

In another party, at another time, or on any other issue, there would have been no argument. But populist Fianna Fáil fifteen months after its last leadership challenge was not like any other party; the national question was no ordinary issue; and Haughey and O'Malley were never likely to agree to differ. Haughey had always mistrusted FitzGerald and felt uneasy about the Forum; he had long been convinced that O'Malley's views were closer to those of the Fine Gael leader than to his, not only on the North but on the economy and on political standards. He had been one of those who objected to unorthodox phone-tapping (of journalists) and the setting-up of colleagues (the O'Donoghue affair).

Now, the answer to the question "Who will rid me of this turbulent priest?" was at hand. O'Malley made public his

67

Des O'Malley expelled from Fianna Fáil Parliamentary Party, May 1984
Derek Spiers/Report

views, first on party discipline and democracy, then on the Forum — he did stand closer to FitzGerald and John Hume than to Haughey — and the business of having him expelled from the Parliamentary Party was set in train immediately. Haughey, fastidious as always when asserting his authority, made sure that there were no legal hitches.

O'Malley now thinks it somewhat ironic that after his major differences with Haughey — on economic issues ranging from public spending to the Gregory deal, on leadership and the presence of low standards in high places — the break between them should have come first on a relatively minor question of party discipline and finally on contraception. It may not have been as strange a business as he thinks. FitzGerald's announcement in September 1981 that he intended to embark on a constitutional crusade challenged Fianna Fáil and reflected at least a temporary shift in Fine Gael: "I want to lead a crusade, a Republican crusade, to make this a genuine Republic..."

It was a vainglorious promise. Several of his own colleagues who grudgingly admired his popularity (and enjoyed the reflected glory) would have preferred to remain forever in opposition rather than advance towards FitzGerald's New Jerusalem under the banner of pluralism.

Vainglorious or not, the promise provoked strong feelings in Fianna Fáil. There was the party's ritual annoyance that anyone should attempt to interfere in the slightest degree with Dev's Constitution, linked with the suspicion — never far from the surface whenever the Constitution was mentioned by "outsiders" — that the claim to jurisdiction over Northern Ireland was about to be abandoned. There was also, somewhere in the background, the uneasy feeling that the party was being put on the spot by being asked to contemplate the removal of sectarian elements from Southern society.

FitzGerald had exposed raw nerves: the national question...
Dev's Constitution... accusations of sectarianism in a
Republic with pretensions to the ideals of Tone and Davis.
As John Hume described it at the opening of the New Ireland
Forum:

The heart of the crisis in Ireland is the conviction —
the profound and seemingly irreducible conviction — of
the majority of Protestants in the North that their ethos
simply would not survive in an Irish political settlement.

Hume asked:

How would we propose to give to Unionists an adequate
sense of security — physical, religious, political, economic
and cultural — in a new Ireland? Are we, the Nationalists
of Ireland, prepared to pay the painful political and
economic price that this will involve? Do we have any idea
of what the price will be? I fear that many of us either
do not, or would prefer not to. The work of the Forum
will forever deprive us of the excuse of either ignorance
or distraction.

But we don't like being deprived of excuses, and that goes
for many of FitzGerald's as well as most of Haughey's
supporters. Their answer to Hume was typically partitionist.
They were not prepared to take any action that would make
Unionists feel more secure. They were not prepared to make
any concessions to pluralism in the South. And if that meant
making the Border a permanent fixture, so be it.

The politics of cultural defence were, with the recession
and the North, our preoccupations of the Eighties. First came
the ban on abortion, writing into the Constitution a
prohibition which already existed in law; then there was the
reform of an unenforceable law on contraception, Haughey's
"Irish solution to an Irish problem"; finally, the rejection
of an attempt to remove the constitutional prohibition on

divorce.

The issues were linked by common themes: Church-State relations and the primacy of the Oireachtas; the role of politicians in the enforcement of morality, and the importance attached by the Republic to the rights of minorities. The debates on all three illuminated attitudes to partition, pluralism, relations with the North and the nature of the Republic. And these were issues on which O'Malley concentrated in the speech he delivered to the Dáil on 20 February 1985. It was, in a way, his valedictory address to Fianna Fáil.

The Bill on which he spoke amended the Act limiting the supply of contraceptives to married people on production of a doctor's prescription. It was opposed by Fianna Fáil and by three members of Fine Gael but was passed with the support of the Workers' Party and Independents. Before and during the debate, lay fundamentalist organisations, some of them called into existence at the time of the abortion referendum, others long accustomed to equally forceful if less public lobbying, exerted considerable pressure on politicians to reject the measure; and their campaign had the support of at least two bishops, Kevin McNamara of Dublin and Jeremiah Newman of Limerick.

As is often the case in such debates, it was not so much the proposal under discussion as the echoes and implications that lent real significance to the affair. O'Malley, pointing out that, with condoms being imported and freely used at a rate of 9 million a year, with supplies openly available in grocery shops in the universities, the Act was not being — and could not be — enforced.

He asked:

> Is it opening the floodgates to try to regularise that? I do not think so, but it's a feature of our national hypocrisy

71

that if the law on the statute book says that things should be one way, it does not matter if things on the ground are different. As long as the law looks all right we cod ourselves into thinking that something that we do not approve of is not happening. Would it not be more sensible to be realistic and look at what is going on around us and realise that, no matter how strongly we might be opposed in principle or in conscience to contraceptives, we would be better to have a law that will be enforced rather than the present situation?

There were certain fundamental matters which far transcended the details of the Bill and which were, in his view, of grave importance to democracy in Ireland: "I cannot ignore the principle that is involved."

He went on:

In the past ten days [since the Bill's publication] the most extraordinary and unprecedented extra-parliamentary pressure has been brought to bear on many members of the House. This is not merely ordinary lobbying. It is far more significant. I regret to have to say that it borders at times almost on the sinister. We have witnessed the public and the private agonies of so many members of the House who are being asked, not to make decisions on this Bill in their own calm and collected judgment, but to make them as a result of emotional, and at times overwhelming, moral pressure. This must constrain their freedom in certain respects.

He pointed out that, under Article 6 of the Constitution, all powers of government derived, under God, from the people, whose right it was to designate the rulers of the State and, in final appeal, to decide all questions of national policy, according to the requirements of the common good. These powers of government were exercisable only by and on the authority of the organs of State established by the Constitution.

The essence of this debate is whether this House agrees with that Article and whether it is prepared to stand firm on it. Article 6 is not often quoted because its provisions are taken for granted, but it cannot be taken for granted today because we must declare whether the people are sovereign.

This debate can be regarded as a sort of watershed in Irish politics. It will have a considerable influence on the whole political, institutional, democratic future, not just of these Twenty-six Counties but of the whole island. We must approach the subject very seriously and bearing that in mind. Is it right to ask ourselves now what would be the reaction and the effect of this Bill being defeated? I am not interested in the reaction or the effect so far as contraception is concerned, because that is no longer relevant. If the Bill is defeated, there are two elements on this island who will rejoice to high heaven. They are the Unionists in Northern Ireland and the extremist Roman Catholics in the Republic.

They are a curious alliance, but they are bound together by the vested interest each of them has in the perpetuation of partition. Neither wishes to know the other. Their wish is to keep this island divided. Most of us here realise that the imposition of partition on this island was a grievous wrong. But its deliberate continuation is equally a grievous wrong. No one who wishes that this island, this race and this nation be united again should try to have that division copperfastened.

It does not matter what any of us might like to say to ourselves about what might be the effects of the availability of condoms or anything else; what really matters and what will matter in ten, twenty or thirty years time is whether the elected representatives of the Irish people decided they wished to underwrite, at least mentally, the concept of partition.

He was not, he confessed, as optimistic as he used to be about the possibility of seeing a Thirty-two County Republic:

I think the day is further away than it might otherwise be because of the events of the last ten or fifteen years. I am certain of one thing in relation to partition — we will never see a Thirty-Two County Republic on this island until, first of all, we have here a Twenty-Six County Republic, in the part we have jurisdiction over today, which is really a Republic, practising real Republican traditions. Otherwise, we can forget about persuading our fellow Irishmen in the North to join us.

"Republican" is perhaps the most abused word in Ireland today... There is an immediate, preconceived notion of what it is. It consists principally of Anglophobia. Mentally, at least, it is an aggressive attitude towards those who do not agree with our views on what the future of this island should be. It consists of turning a blind eye to violence, seeing no immorality, often, in the most awful violence, seeing immorality only in one area, the area with which this Bill deals.

Often, it is displayed by letting off steam in the fifteen minutes before closing time with some rousing ballad that makes one vaguely feel good and gets one clapped on the back by people who are stupid enough to think that that sort of flag waving is the way to make progress in this island — to go back into your own trenches rather than try to reach out to people whom we need to reach.

He was distressed by the evident lack of trust in young people, both inside and outside the Dáil:

Young people can hardly be blamed if they look at this House and its members with a certain cynicism, because they see here a certain hypocrisy... If I were to place my trust anywhere today, before God I would place it in the young people. I would not abuse or defame them, by implication at least, in the way in which they have been defamed as people who are incapable of making any kind of sound judgment unless it is legislated for them. Even the exercise of their own private consciences must be something that must be legislated for. I have said before that I cannot accept that concept, though I have seen a reverend bishop saying that we can legislate for private morality. I beg to take issue with him.

Technically, of course, he is right. I can think of at least two countries in the world where private morality is legislated for. One is Iran and the other is Pakistan. Private morality is enforced by public flogging every day in Teheran and other cities in Iran. It takes place in Pakistan where every political party has been dissolved except the government party. One aspect of the enforcement of private morality in these countries is the stoning to death of adulteresses. I do not know what happens to adulterers, but adulteresses get stoned to death.

In a democratic republic, people should not think in terms of having laws other than those that allow citizens to make their own free choice insofar as these private matters are concerned. That is what I believe a republic should do. It should take account of the reasonable views of all groups, including all minorities, because if we do not take into account the rights of minorities here can we complain if they are not taken into account in the other part of this island, or anywhere else? The rights of minorities are not taken into account in Iran — the Bahai are murdered at the rate of dozens a week because they will not subscribe to the dictat of Islam. I do not say that will happen here, but it is the kind of slippery slope we are on.

The tragedy is that so far as morality, public or private, is concerned, the only aspect of it that agitates us is sexual morality or things that have to do with it. Could any other issue get things so worked up here as something like this? Do we not need to remind ourselves that God gave Moses nine other Commandants and the other nine are numbered through five and seven through ten, as the Americans say.

In support of the case for pluralism, O'Malley quoted some passages from an address delivered by Mario Cuomo, the Governor of New York, on the subject of religious belief and public morality as perceived by a Catholic politician. Cuomo had said:

The Catholic public official lives the political truth most Catholics through most of American history have accepted and insisted on — the truth that to assure our freedom we must allow others the same freedom, even if it occasionally produces conduct by them which, for us, would be sinful... Catholics must practise the teachings of Christ... not just by trying to make laws for others to live by, but by living the laws already written for us by God.

We can be fully Catholic; clearly, proudly, totally at ease with ourselves, a people in the world, transforming it, a light to this nation. Appealing to the best in our people, not the worst. Persuading not coercing. Leading people to truth by love and still, all the while, respecting and enjoying our unique pluralistic democracy. And we can do it even as politicians.

Cuomo's speech had been described by a Jesuit professor

at Fordham University as a milestone in the history of the American Church. But O'Malley commented:

> If he were to deliver that address in this country in the last ten days, I know the answer he would get... I believe that the truth lies in the kind of attitude that that man takes and in the way that he recognises how any Roman Catholic legislator or governor must operate in a pluralist society. Does the House notice the way he talks proudly of pluralism? It is a bad word here. You are supposed to be ashamed of wanting to see a pluralist society in this country. You are supposed not to want that, but to want one which is dominated by one form of thinking only. There are Unionists in the North who want the same. While both of us are that way, we can assure ourselves that never the twain shall meet.

The Forum report had contained a spirit of reconciliation and openness, a recognition of what needed to be done to show the people of Northern Ireland that they need not fear for what they called their civil and religious liberties. But if the Dáil rejected the Bill it was discussing, could they be persuaded other than that the Forum report meant nothing — "that it was a bag of wind, a lot of words"? Could the spirit, as well as the letter of the report, be cast aside?

Said O'Malley:

> I am concerned not just about the Unionists in Northern Ireland. I am concerned also about the position, in the context of this debate, of the Roman Catholics in Northern Ireland and I know something about them. I married one of them twenty years ago on this very day, 20 February 1965; and I know a lot of them. I cannot accept, going on the statements that were so freely made inside and outside this House, that in any country or jurisdiction where there was availability of contraceptives on the lines

77

suggested in this Bill the people would immediately become degenerate. They are not degenerate in Northern Ireland and they have had for very many years full access to any form of contraception they wanted, at any time and at any age, in any marital condition.

Contraceptives had been made freely available in the North when Paddy Devlin was Minister of Health and Social Services in the power-sharing Executive:

Not one word was spoken in Northern Ireland at that time in relation to something which was way beyond anything which is proposed here. Why is it that if something is all right in Co.Armagh, half of that is an abomination in Co. Louth? Is that logical, or is there some deeper explanation for it? I think that there must be some deeper explanation for it, because it is not logical. Why should the suggested standards for individual Roman Catholics be so different a few miles apart? I cannot follow it. As an indication of the fact that the statements made about the appalling effect of what is suggested are wrong, there is the living proof of the strength of Northern Ireland's Catholics to stand up for themselves and make their own decision and not be regarded as people who are so weak that they need public legislation in order to keep them from sin.

The SDLP, O'Malley claimed, was acutely embarrassed at what was happening in the Republic. The party knew that all of the effort they had put into the Forum and their belief in it was mocked by the controversy in the South. And he recalled another such controversy, over the Mother and Child scheme in 1951. Admitting that he had only lately read the full account of the Dáil debate for the first time, he commented:

It is incredible that members of this House and of the

government of the day could be as craven and supine as they were, as we look back at them now. It shows how much the atmosphere has changed... Then, one has to ask oneself "has the atmosphere changed?" Because when the chips are down, is it going to be any different?

He had mentioned a supine Coalition; he might have added an opportunistic Fianna Fáil. Dev's only contribution to the 1951 debate had been: "We have heard enough." When the chips were down in 1985 things were no different.

A month earlier, at a conference in Kylemore Abbey, O'Malley had made public his views on Church-State relations. In *The Irish Times* Michael Finlan had reported how he'd been applauded for those views. But no sooner had Finlan left to telephone his report than the criticism began. Now O'Malley said:

This whole matter affects me personally and politically. I have thought about it and agonised about it. Quite a number of Deputies have been subjected to a particular type of pressure. But I am possibly unique in that I have been subjected to two enormous pressures, the more general type and a particular political one. They are both like floodtides — neither of them is easy to resist and it is probably more than twice as hard to resist the two of them.

But it comes down to certain fundamentals. One has to take into account everything that has been said but one must act in accordance with one's conscience, not on contraceptives, which is irrelevant now, but on the bigger and deeper issues that I have talked about today.

I cannot avoid acting, especially in my present situation where I do not have the protection of the Whip, other than in the way I feel, giving some practical recognition at least to the kind of pressures and the entreaties of friends for

79

my own good, which I greatly appreciate.

I will conclude by quoting from a letter in *The Irish Times* of 16 February signed by Fr Dominic Johnson, O.S.B., a monk of Glenstal Abbey, where he says: "With respect to Mr O'Malley, he might reflect with profit on the life of St Thomas More, who put his conscience before politics and lost his life for doing so."

The politics of this would be very easy. The politics would be, to be one of the lads, the safest way in Ireland. But I do not believe that the interests of this State, of our Constitution and of this Republic, would be served by putting politics before conscience in regard to this. There is a choice of a kind that can only be answered by saying that I stand by the Republic and accordingly I will not oppose this Bill.

The Bill passed by 83 votes to 80. O'Malley was not present in the Dáil when the vote was taken, so that, technically, he did not even abstain. And since he was no longer a member of Fianna Fáil's Parliamentary Party, he could not be considered subject to the party Whip. But the point of his speech was not lost on Fianna Fáil or its leader: O'Malley was given three days in which to say why he should not be expelled from the organisation.

Barry Desmond, the Minister for Health, called his contribution "the finest I have heard in thirteen years in the Dáil" and *The Irish Times,* in an editorial, commented:

It is a measure of the unreality of much that passes for politics in this State that a perfectly respectable speech should be hailed as if [O'Malley] were bringing down wisdom from heaven. He actually voiced Republican sentiments... and spoke as if he meant it; which he manifestly did. This is not in any way to decry the sincerity of Mr O'Malley but simply to mark the extent to which the former Republican party has become the cautious, mind-you-I've-said-nothing party. The Government... have been the Republicans.

Fianna Fáil's anger was explained by an un-named Deputy who said: "The feeling was that we would have won had he decided to support us and bring a few others with him." On 26 February, Haughey recommended his expulsion to the National Executive. After a discussion lasting three and a half hours, the vote was 73 to 9 in favour of this course of action. Lenihan said it was an example of democracy at its best. The charge was: conduct unbecoming a member of Fianna Fáil.

Progressive Democrats

O'MALLEY WAS NOW to all intents and purposes on his own. His departure from Fianna Fáil was not, as some had predicted, the signal for others to resign. Lynch's opinion on the day of his expulsion that here was a man whose views would find an echo in the hearts and minds of party members throughout the country seemed to have been based more on hope than on reality. Such complaints as arose from the ranks were muted and came slowly to the surface. When opinion polls began to show a drop in Haughey's popularity, his spokesmen said firmly that such a response had been anticipated. They had braced themselves for it and were satisfied that the damage done was containable. After a radio interview in which he clumsily agreed that he had long been of the opinion that Haughey was unfit to govern, O'Malley himself fell silent. John Kelly of Fine Gael was to talk of him, in a characteristic phrase, as having been "marginalised" and set to "sleeping under (political) bridges".

O'Malley admits that the break with the party in which he had spent all of his political life affected him deeply. He felt cut off, needlessly, from people who had for years been both colleagues and friends. For the first time in over fifty years, he remarked ruefully, the O'Malley name was missing from the list of Fianna Fáil's public representatives in Limerick. But the city remained loyal, demonstrating on his return a fierce combination of local pride and resentment. He was urged privately to set up a new party immediately, now that the break was final and irrevocable. He counselled caution. Both he and his supporters needed time to make up their minds in an atmosphere free of the excitement which his expulsion had provoked. He was prepared to take his own, much-quoted advice: "Let the hare sit." Gradually, the speculation about a new party died down and meetings in Leinster House or its environs of what remained of "The Club of 22" (those who had voted against Haughey in the second of the three challenges to his leadership) went unremarked.

Under the calming influence of his wife, Pat, he began to sift through the messages that arrived from other constituencies, mostly from old Fianna Fáil supporters but also from members of other parties who admired the tone and content of his "I stand by the Republic" speech. He was wary of this admiration and slow to accept invitations to speak; anxious to avoid raising expectations which, when the hard choice came, might turn out to have been the result of nothing more than a temporary mood. It took several months of discussion with Mary Harney, his Limerick loyalists and others from Cork, Carlow, Dublin and the West before he became convinced that a New Departure was a realistic prospect. A serious car crash in November had him in hospital for weeks; it delayed the discussions but precipitated the decision.

Kevin D. O'Connor dramatised the events in a piece he wrote for the *Sunday Independent:*

> The injuries he sustained faced him up to the issue he had been dodging the previous months... This time in hospital was a breathing-space for calm calculation of options. As O'Malley pondered the pros and cons, the weight of evidence accumulated. A private poll commissioned by Cork associates had shown 39 per cent in favour of a new party led by O'Malley. Fianna Fáil reaction to the Anglo-Irish Accord threw a fresh swathe of supporters in his path...
>
> He had run out of excuses to say "No." Especially to Mary Harney. All through the summer she had nagged him to move, move, move. A persistent, idealistic intriguer who represented in her persona the young disaffection that would harness the future, she had urged him to act before the year was out. "If you don't do it before the end of the year — it will be an eternity afterwards."

There were others whom O'Connor described as midwives to the birth of the new party. Michael McDowell, a grandson of Eoin MacNeill, had been chairman of FitzGerald's constituency organisation and his personal director of elections. On the night of O'Malley's expulsion he wrote offering his services. Like Harney, he urged a New Departure. So did Paul MacKay and Barra O Tuama of Cork,

**O'Malley leaving Leinster House after his expulsion from the
Fianna Fáil Parliamentary Party, with Mary Harney TD**

Derek Spiers/Report

**Des O'Malley, Mary Harney and Michael Keating at PD meeting,
April 1986**
Derek Spiers/Report

businessmen who had supported Lynch; Michael Kearns of Carlow and John Quinn of Limerick, powerful local activists in the Fianna Fáil organisation. They chose the title Progressive Democrats because, as O'Connor wrote:

It summed up what they felt the new party should be about. McDowell, in particular, was keen on what he calls "participation" in State activity by citizens. Harney and O'Malley had already been skewered on the flag of "democracy" in their previous careers. Both were intent on progressive social policies, especially Harney, whose daily political life faced the awesome realities of Corporation housing estates.

There was no advertising agency involved, no marketing whizz-kids. Instead, the title was sent down the line to Carlow and Limerick and Tallaght and test-marketed informally among groups of supporters. The word back was favourable, emphatically so from Tallaght. Harney said: "It just goes to show you're better off relying on your own instincts, your own judgment."

If there was any hesitation about launching the party before the end of the year, it was removed by the signing of the Anglo-Irish Agreement at Hillsborough in mid-November and Haughey's unfavourable and, as it turned out, unpopular reaction to it. O'Malley, in line with his speeches at Scariff and in the Dáil, favoured the Agreement and believed that Haughey's reaction would be interpreted as, at best, opportunistic. (This was the issue that provoked Harney's break with the party.) And in spite of the Agreement the signs of recovery in the fortunes of Fine Gael and Labour were slight. There would never be a better time.

At the launching of the new party on Saturday 21 December O'Malley said:

The high hopes we held in the past and our belief in

ourselves as a strong and independent nation have been replaced by a crisis of confidence, evidenced by rising unemployment and emigration and the fact that national morale is at an all-time low.

Two generations have passed since the present shape of Irish politics emerged. In those sixty years, such democracy has borne the marks of division, hostility and suspicion based less on our vision of the future than our view of the past. Whatever logic there was in those divisions, there is none today.

But this generation of Irishmen and women would no longer accept the legacy of division that history had given us:

For the past year I have been struck by the strength of feeling throughout the country in favour of breaking the moulds of Irish politics and giving the Irish voters a new and real alternative. I believe that the old loyalties on which the present parties feed are no longer enough to sustain them...

I believe that there is a great concensus in Ireland which favours a peaceful approach to the problem in Northern Ireland; which favours fundamental tax reform; which favours enterprise; which favours a clear distinction between Church and State. ...Irish politics must be transformed. Experience tells me that no such transformation will come from within the existing parties. It must come from outside. There must be a new beginning.

Pointing to "the great paradox that parties which are divided by so little depend for their survival on ruthless supression of internal debate," he addressed himself to "all democrats of goodwill who share my beliefs and my confidence that the face of Irish politics *can* be transformed."

He refused to describe his announcement as the launching

of the new party but, that, in fact, was what it was.

The heady round of packed meetings and rushing applicants began almost immediately. Lynch came up with an endorsement of "this new dimension in public life." The headquarters at South Frederick Street in Dublin were overwhelmed with messages of encouragement, offers of help and money, callers who had never before set foot in a party's offices or imagined themselves playing a part in political affairs.

Ironically, it seemed as if O'Malley's years of attempting to initiate a debate about the nature and direction of politics had suddenly borne fruit; ironically, because the harvest was now fraught with risks. The enthusiasm might still be short-lived, a simplistic reaction reflecting frustration with the established parties — specifically with Fianna Fáil's attitude to the Anglo-Irish Agreement and the Coalition's handling of the economy. The original poll which showed almost 40 per cent of the electorate in favour of a new party had been conducted eight months earlier: would the mood hold?

Joseph O'Malley in the *Sunday Independent* struck a cautionary note on the morning after the new party was announced. He wrote:

For Des O'Malley the new challenge is to buck the political trend which shows, with one exception in recent times, that new parties start well but finish badly. The post-war history offers little consolation to those attempting to break the mould of Irish politics... Today, realistically, the best that any new party can probably hope is to hold the balance of power in a tight electoral contest.

This, in a sense, was what the *Irish Press* suspected O'Malley was about:

His main emphasis in what he has had to say has been on the style of leadership of Mr Haughey, the way in which

Mr Haughey dominates party thinking and the way in which the party has, according to Mr O'Malley, opted for political opportunism on occasions. The basis for the new party, to judge from this analysis, seems more one of personality than principle.

The paper's political correspondent, Sean O'Rourke, believed that O'Malley's major task would lie in convincing people that his party's primary relevance was not "to prevent Charles Haughey from becoming Taoiseach after the next General Election."

In the *Irish Independent* Stephen O'Byrnes, then the paper's News Analysis Editor, now the Progressive Democrats' Director of Policy and Press Relations, made a more positive suggestion:

Provided O'Malley's party can prove equal to the task of responding credibly to voter dissatisfaction, they can become a durable and substantial political force. Meantime, it looks as if they will continue at least to attract the disillusioned from the ranks of the other main parties.

That was, indeed, what was beginning to happen. On 11 January, at a meeting in Cork which was attended by 3,000 people, Pearse Wyse, the city's senior Fianna Fáil Deputy joined them. Less than two weeks later, at an even bigger meeting in Galway, his colleague, Bobby Molloy joined. And on 8 April, Michael Keating became the first Fine Gael Deputy to enter their ranks. Two Labour Senators, Timmy Conway of Kildare and Helena McAuliffe-Ennis of Longford-Westmeath completed the parliamentary group.

Support in the opinion polls fluctuated wildly. In mid-January, it stood at 19 per cent, leading Chris Glennon, the political correspondent of the *Irish Independent*, to write that the party had radically altered the country's political structure. By early February, at 25 per cent, it was ahead of both Fine Gael and Labour. But before the month was out it had dropped to 20 per cent and by mid-April to 16 per cent. It was still sufficiently strong to worry the established parties.

Early in the year, FitzGerald acknowledged that the emergence of the Progressive Democrats would have a fundamental impact on politics even if, as he believed, its support in a General Election turned out to be significantly lower than in the original polls. He placed the party in the category of classic European liberalism — rejecting State intervention on both economic and social issues — and saw its emergence as not particularly surprising:

In a situation of grave economic difficulty, where the level of public expenditure is disproportionate to resources and the tax burden is correspondingly high and where, for demographic as well as external reasons, you have a very high level of unemployment, any party system is going to evoke a high level of dissatisfaction.

With the additional problems of alienation and increasing volatility, "one would have expected a new element in the party structure to arise spontaneously." Nor did he find it surprising that the new element should have come from Fianna Fáil which, in his view, was now "fixated on retaining existing support in the older age groups — a fixation reflected in its attitude to social as well as Northern policy."

He accepted the evidence of the polls that the Progressive Democrats would draw popular support from both Fianna Fáil and Fine Gael but insisted that the Fine Gael departures were less permanent:

Moving towards an election there will be a much greater tendency for people in Fine Gael to return to their original allegiance. Antipathy to the Fianna Fáil leadership is far stronger in the PD than any resistance to Fine Gael or

91

Labour. So the Fine Gael people are more likely to return than the Fianna Fáil people are.

The political geography of the country, however, would help to determine how defections by their supporters affected the disposition of the parties' seats:

It could even be that as many Fine Gael seats as Fianna Fáil seats are eventually at risk.

And there was another qualification:

Unless the PD commits itself firmly to the Right, it will have increasing difficulty saying in what way it differs from Fine Gael as it approaches an election.

Lenihan's dismissive "flash-in-the-pan" was characteristic of Fianna Fáil's reaction. He found it predictable that the people most affected by the Republic's problems should be those, from late 20s to early 50s, who made up most of the audiences at the meetings and rallies of the new party:

They are worried about their own jobs, about children coming on — getting education and work for them — and about the future generally. All that is translated into political radicalism. But it's no way of settling their problems. Given their frustrations and insecurity, it is a predictable, psychological reaction.

The showing of the Progressive Democrats in the polls was "a temporary response" — a reaction to insecurity over jobs and taxation. The last time that this kind of thing had happened was in the 1950s when people emigrated without hope, but said Lenihan:

Times are different now. The radical attitude of this period reflects a mood of the Right rather than the Left and I find that very disturbing. It's a negative rather than a positive response. The only end product of Right-wing radicalism is destabilisation of the political system, leading to class antagonism, which we have never had here. It's

92

based on extreme *laissez faire*, selfish materialism which takes no cognisance of the weak, deprived and less-well-off in our society.

If Lenihan worried about the emergence of class politics, Labour and the Workers' Party welcomed it. For Labour in particular, the arrival of the Progressive Democrats presented an opportunity to escape from one of the snares of Coalition — its own loss of identity.

For three years the party had had to watch the Ps and Qs of partnership. Speeches, statements and interviews had been measured in two ways: what they conveyed to Labour's supporters and activists on the ground and what they conveyed to Fine Gael. Now, Dick Spring could launch an attack on those who would protect businessmen and the self-employed from the ravages of public spending without leaving himself open to an interpretation to which John Bruton felt bound to respond. He could declare that a high level of public expenditure was necessary to continue the essential task of redistribution without provoking the ire of Fine Gael backbenchers. This was what he meant when he said that the Progressive Democrats would make easier the task of clarifying Labour's role in a critical period.

Like FitzGerald, Spring was anxious to underline the dislocation in Fianna Fáil. He said:

It will break the Fianna Fáil monolith that has dominated Irish politics since the Twenties. I don't think you are going to get any more the national loyalty that Dev, Lemass and, for a time, Lynch commanded. People are already breaking free of the old loyalties. They are going to start demanding freedom on social issues, too — the kind of freedom the parties have not been prepared to admit that they want.

O'Malley reacted indignantly to the suggestion that the

party derived its philosophies from the Right or that it was a classic liberal party in the European mould. He complained about the Irish obsession with trying to classify everything in terms that might be appropriate elsewhere but were not appropriate here:

> The categories are not necessarily Irish categories. They tend to be British or continental European and I don't think one can easily define what we are doing in those terms. Ideological demarcation simply does not apply in the way it does in those countries and I reject this attempted classification. What is needed here is a pragmatic response to a series of very severe problems and you can't classify that in a theoretical way.

He is even more indignant about the perceptions of the party's support as more or less middle-aged and middle class:

> The public opinion polls contradict that. We get support everywhere, from all classes and groups. Because you have higher support in one group than in others doesn't mean that you have no support outside that category... Anyway, categorising people by class is basically alien to this society.

O'Malley's reluctance to accept any label is equalled only by the eagerness of others to pin one on him. Middle class, monetarist, old style liberal or the latest Fianna Fáil offshoot — all rejected as tags which are either irrelevant or inaccurate or both. He does, however, acknowledge the similarities between the foundation of the Progressive Democrats and the foundation of Fianna Fáil:

> Fianna Fáil was set up in reaction to the Civil War. Its founders opposed those, the majority in Sinn Féin, who were saying essentially that the Civil War should continue, that people should look to the past. Fianna Fáil looked to the future. Now, we are beginning to confront our own problems in the context of the present and future rather

than in the context of the old Civil War divisions — the past.

De Valera in the Twenties had urged his followers to "face facts." It was his way of saying that, whether they liked it or not, the Free State had been accepted by the majority of the electorate and their job was to gain control of it. To do this, they had to take some steps which they might have considered unpalatable, such as entering the Dáil and competing electorally with Cumann na nGaedhal. They had taken those steps and made their own of the State. In the Fifties, Lemass had faced the fact that, without an industrial revolution, the State would bleed to death. He had inspired a revolution and ensured its survival. Neither de Valera nor Lemass had been afraid to change his mind when circumstances demanded change. O'Malley believed in following that example.

Over the years, he had changed his attitude to social issues, the North and nuclear energy. At his first national conference in May he said:

To exclude new evidence, new understanding from our consideration is not a recipe for progress. Sadly I must say that one of the bedevilling features of our public life in Ireland is that too often blind prejudice is confused with consistency, while the virtue of open-mindedness is confused with uncertainty. With the speed of change today, the closed mind is inevitably the false anchor of the insecure.

The conference revealed a degree of open-mindedness which other parties would certainly have refused to tolerate. Issues were debated with a seriousness normally associated with organisations of the Left. Most of the delegates, young to middle-aged, were articulate, well-informed, unemotional. They were prepared to cross swords with the platform around which the cult of personality was markedly absent. Enterprise and self-reliance were themes that appealed to them: when they discussed the black economy their indignation was directed, not so much at tax avoidance and evasion, but at the reasons for it — the tax system itself. They were deeply critical of the Government, particularly on economic and financial matters and scarcely, if ever, mentioned Fianna Fáil. The social issue which concerned them most was divorce. This was predictable enough, partly because a referendum on the constitutional prohibition was now under way; and the Progressive Democrats could claim that they had influenced the Government's decision to hold it. Concern about their popularity had reminded FitzGerald and Fine Gael of their commitments on two fronts: financial rectitude and social reform. FitzGerald's response to the first was to place Bruton in the Department of Finance in spite of the antagonism the move was bound to provoke in the ranks of the Labour Party. The referendum was his response to the second.

If the conference, and O'Malley's address in particular, evoked memories of FitzGerald's early years as leader of Fine Gael, when that party embarked on a social democratic route, the referendum on divorce put a damper on rash expectations of headlong change. Where the "constitutional crusade" had foundered, the divorce proposal perished on the rocks of Catholic fundamentalism and Fianna Fáil resistance.

The pattern of the 1983 referendum was reproduced more faithfully than the proponents of change thought possible. It was still a case of Dublin versus the rest, reminding Tom Garvin of the medieval Pale; the young, who had been generally expected to give the proposal substantial support, obviously did not. The cultural defenders had mounted a superior campaign from pulpit and platform; and insecurity and fear had proved a more potent force than appeals to generosity, liberalism or the spirit of the Republic.

The Progressive Democrats, fresh from the triumph of their conference, learned that breaking the moulds of Irish politics would be a long, hard slog. The party by now claimed a membership of more than 20,000 and organisations in most of the 41 constituencies. But, whether because of the inexperience of its activists or the uncertainty of its supporters, it failed to make any appreciable impact on the vote in all but a few areas. Similar complaints were laid against many local Fine Gael and, in some places, Labour branches. For the new party, as for many would be reformers, it was a salutary lesson in the realities of Irish life.

The New Leader

O'MALLEY IS A politician who reacts to a changing climate rather than one who creates the climate for change. The same could be said of nearly all Irish politicians, but over the years he has come to react with more agility than most and, in spite of a mellowing personality, with increasing impatience at the reluctance of the rest to face new circumstances until they become overwhelming.

He was never an easy practitioner (and is now the sworn enemy) of the head-down, wink-and-nod, mind-you-I've-said-nothing style of politics, if only because he never quite dropped the habit of calling a spade a spade and, now that he leads a party of his own, has one less reason to be circumspect. His frankness about his own changes of direction, as much as the gradually discovered vision of a country free of cant and evasion, contributes to a fresh and lively image, grafted to the steel of experience gained in a tough school. The impression is created of a man who knows what he wants but knows, too, how hard it will be to get it.

He finds depressing evidence of the reluctance to face facts in the Coalition's attitude to the nation's finances, now so precarious as to endanger independence (his view) and in the refusal of Fianna Fáil and the agents of Catholic fundamentalism to accept the need for social reform. He may object to ideological tags, but the changes in Irish society to which his present stance and the emergence of the Progressive Democrats are attributable can be easily traced.

The changes began with Lemass's industrial revolution and became more acute as a new, largely urban society replaced de Valera's rural certainties. In a different sphere, they had their origins in Lemass's new approach to the North. The social and economic changes accelerated with the prosperity of the Seventies. Membership of the EEC gave it an international dimension and increasing access to information about events elsewhere, via television and broader press coverage, presented a matching cultural challenge for which we were equally unprepared. The explosion of the Northern conflict at the end of the Sixties challenged old assumptions about the national question and lent new urgency to the adoption of a more realistic approach. The protection of the Southern State, on the one hand; recognition of Unionist resistance, on the other, called for an abandonment of gratifying rhetoric and the postures that went with it. They were replaced not so much by a policy as by pragmatism, from which there were two departures in attempts to devise a long-term solution; the first at Sunningdale, the second at Hillsborough.

Unnoticed by all but a few sociologists and economists, industrial and demographic changes in the South were breaking long-established moulds. They, however, did not begin to impinge on the minds of politicians or policy-makers until the deep, and apparently paralysing, recession of the Eighties made recognition unavoidable. By then, the conversion of a settled, largely rural society into a fragmented urban society was well under way. New patterns were taking shape, new demands being made, new attitudes being formed. In twenty years, Irish society has changed more rapidly and more fundamentally than that of any other developing country; and few, if any, of the changes that have taken place have been planned, even in the most rudimentary way.

Lemass's revolution worked, but what at first had seemed a painless transition was to produce its own set of problems. It gave us a new vocabulary, freed us from an obsession with our ensnaring past, brought us face to face with the modern world. But there was a grievous lack of planning, a failure to recognise that growth without social engineering, economic advance without regard to the cultural and environmental consequences, were bound to exacerbate the difficulties with our identity which had begun to emerge almost as soon as we had gained independence.

As the decay of inner cities was accompanied by the drab, irregular march of much of our suburban housing, so the destruction of settled communities was accompanied by the growth of areas which had no communal centre at all. Industrial sites were chosen, often at the whim of the industrialist or to satisfy the need of some local politician, with little care for their social and environmental impact.

More students than ever passed through secondary and technical schools, but no one could be sure where, or if, jobs could be found for them. And they were luckier than those who had left school earlier: as unemployment climbed from 5 per cent in 1962 to 18 per cent in 1986, those most seriously affected were the unskilled who tended to follow their parents to the dole queues.

O'Malley and the Progressive Democrats defied the conventional wisdom of the previous decade which presumed that such circumstances would provoke an irresistible surge to the Left by impatient youth. There was, indeed, a surge but not (for the most part) by impatient youth and certainly not to the Left. It came from the middle classes, allowing that the term embraces many who might be called working class but would not answer to the name and it came from people who, if they did not care for the label Right, would agree with those root-and-branch economists who for several years had been complaining about lame ducks, white elephants and other expensive animals among the semi-State companies.

They were people who had taken part in the PAYE protests of the late Seventies and had seen no return on their efforts. People who were buying their houses, worrying about their childrens' future, resenting the share of their earnings which they paid to the State. People who, in other circumstances, might be supporting Fianna Fáil or Fine Gael. Now, their slogan could well be: what we have we hold.

But that's very far from the whole picture. The articulate, highly educated and much travelled generation that has grown up since Lemass's revolution is, in many ways, more generous than the old. It is certainly more tolerant, more fair minded and more independent. If it does not yet command a majority, it is only a matter of time until it does.

O'Malley makes a direct appeal to the generosity of this generation. And it's here, perhaps more than in their economic policies, that the Progressive Democrats come face to face with old fears and prejudices.

On the day after the divorce referendum, Tom Garvin, in his commentary in the *Irish Press* noted how one of the changes of the last ten years had been the re-emergence of specifically Catholic and what he called "even pulpit politics." He wrote:

This has been, in part, in reaction to — or even anticipation of — pressure for liberalisation of our laws, coming from very articulate liberal and radical groups based on working class and middle class sentiment in Dublin and the bigger towns.

The Catholic Church historically has stayed out of active politics since the Twenties. This was partly due to fear of the bitterness over the Treaty split of 1922 affecting the Church itself, as it had so much of Irish society. It was due, of course, also to the willingness of democratic political leaders to accept Catholic ideals of social organisations. Politicians generally supported traditional Catholic values; there was, therefore, little need for clerical or lay Catholic action in the political arena.

This situation has been changing for some time. The old Free State versus Republic bitterness has faded and is, for most people, only an historical memory. Thus, the old inhibition against involvement in electoral politics, once seen as the monopoly of the parties, has faded. The growth of anti-traditional opinions among many younger politicians, journalists, academics and public officials has increased the temptation to engage in what amounts to politics of cultural defence.

Garvin described cultural defence as an instinct of collective self-preservation rather than anti-Protestant bigotry or Anglophobia. But, given the sizes of the majorities in the two referenda, "one must seriously question the sensitivity of some of our political leaders to the minds and the everyday concerns of the majority of the Irish people."

Partition had often been represented by nationalists as having been a bad thing, but from the point of view of the politics of cultural defence, it could be said to have given Irish Catholicism the best of both worlds; in particular, an opportunity to keep most of Irish society in the mould favoured by most Catholic lay and clerical leaders since 1922.

Garvin wrote:

All this referendum has done is to give those of us who forgot this elementary fact of Irish political life a salutary reminder. We are not living in post-Christian England, and Irish independence has really made a difference, although scarcely the difference wished for by some Republicans.

Clearly, if O'Malley faced a challenge from the Left on his economic and financial attitudes, he faced an even sterner challenge from the Right when it came to social issues. But he was beginning to establish his own constituency and he was not to be shifted from the view that he had expressed with such conviction at the close of his address to the national conference: "Time and tide are on our side." Nor was he about to revoke the commitment he had made in his speech on contraception when he said: "If I were to place my trust anywhere today, before God I would place it in the young people."

The changes that were taking place might be ragged and uneven and there were times when the process of modernisation appeared to have ground to a halt. But no change had been easy: it had taken Lemass almost thirty years to get into a position where he could wean Fianna Fáil away from the futile pursuit of economic nationalism. Would he have succeeded, even then, if it had not been for the threat of virtual extinction? The country had recovered, slowly and painfully, from the wounds inflicted on it by the debacle of the Mother and Child scheme in the Fifties; but it had recovered. Fianna Fáil and the State had come under threat when the arms crisis broke in 1970 and Lynch had been put to the pin of his collar to save both. And if all of this had the ring of crisis management about it, perhaps we would now get the message that there must be a better way.

O'Malley also looks outside Ireland for example and consolation. To Mario Cuomo, the Governor of New York State whom he respects as a highly successful Catholic politician in a pluralist society. He agrees with him on most social issues — abortion is the exception, Cuomo supports it — and probably finds echoes of his own thinking in the Governor's statement:

> We can offer more to people than ever before. Not handouts, but what they want above all else — the chance to earn their own way with hope and dignity.

He dislikes comparison with David Owen's SDP in Britain, but has high admiration for another Social Democrat, Helmut Schmidt, the former Chancellor of West Germany:

> He was extraordinarily adept at handling very tricky problems. It was not just a matter of running an economy and a successful economy at that; the Germans have very difficult relations with East Germany and the East generally and I thought he handled those extremely skilfully. In domestic affairs and in the EEC he was extraordinarily successful — probably the most successful of all Chancellors after Adenauer.

What probably appeals most to O'Malley in both Cuomo

and Schmidt is their ability to make up their own minds, to reconcile opposing forces and to get things done. He would like to see more Irish people looking to countries other than Britain for example. Calling himself a post-conciliar Catholic, who could no longer see himself fitting into pre-conciliar attitudes, he believes, whatever the evidence of the referenda, that an increasing number of people have managed to escape from the restrictions of the past.

Looking back on the Fifties and the city of his youth, he feels as if he were looking into another century. Under the influence of industrial development, Shannon, the NIHE and the arrival of people from other countries and other parts of Ireland, the city has shed its authoritarian image and found new horizons. Steve Coughlan had been replaced by Jim Kemmy of the Democratic Socialists as the representative of the Left. Limerick is Ireland in microcosm:

> People used to think in terms of the Catholic Church only as they saw it in Ireland. They had very little experience of Catholicism elsewhere. It's a very different matter now. You can console yourself with a quite different approach that's being taken by the Catholic Church in other countries. I would find it hard to believe that the Irish Catholic church has a monopoly of wisdom and everyone else is out of step.

O'Malley himself has been accused of releasing reservoirs of resentment against the old ways, religious and political. He insists that the old ways have failed and that new circumstances demand new responses:

> My definition of political integrity includes the requirement to adapt politically to new situations. Much has changed in this country throughout my tenure in active politics. The age profile of the population is very different; the general level of education is much higher than it was

Des O'Malley with his wife, Pat, April 1986   Derek Spiers/Report

The Progressive Democrats' first party conference, May 1986
Derek Spiers/Report

107

twenty years ago; we are much more exposed to a variety of outside pressures, social, economic and political. Irish people are now better able and have the means to articulate their needs and their concerns. Regrettably, we politicians do not listen often enough or closely enough to what our electorates are telling us ...

Everyone who joins this party must do so with an open mind... If this means that some of us must depart from previously stated views — so be it. I personally refuse to be a hostage to history, no matter how recent, if my instincts tell me that new policies and new directions are needed.

To the accusations of the Left that he is intent on destroying the welfare system, he replies:

I resent and flatly reject the claim that my party is espousing a policy of reducing social welfare and screwing the poor. Unlike the Labour Party which would appear to want to see the Irish people all equally miserable, our philosophy is to improve the lot of all our people. Yes, we applaud and will encourage initiative and enterprise because that is the way to create real jobs ...

But far from turning our backs on the poor and disadvantaged, we stand for a better level of services to those really in need. And that requires better delivery of services, which in too many cases at present are dispersed unfairly to all.

Accused of reneging on nationalism, he replies with a portrait of the fireside, armchair or bar stool patriot:

This kind of rhetorical patriot finds his political counterpart in those politicians who are strong on flag waving, big on the need for a Thirty-two County united Ireland now and at any cost and heavily into ritual incantations of the dead generations with Wolfe Tone and

1798 top of the Republican pops. These politicians are so wrapped up in the need to score political points over opponents, and so obsessed with blaming every ill in Irish society on the absence of unity, that the national question is reduced to the status of a political football. Getting fair treatment for Northern Nationalists or ensuring that the environment for jobs in the North improves is no part of such an agenda. The wrap the green flag round me brigade in the South would do well to realise that neither they nor their attitudes ever put coal on a Nationalist fire North of the Border, dinner on a Nationalist table or slates on a Nationalist roof.

At a meeting of the SDLP in Belfast, he presented a contrasting protrait of such Republicans as John Hume and Seamus Mallon:

> People of enormous personal courage and integrity... believing that constitutional politics is the only way forward... the kind of Republican who rejects the simplistic notion that in some unspecified way unity is just around the corner if only the right personalities were there to lead. This is the kind of Republican who sees and appreciates that any unity of political purpose on this island can only come through respecting the diversity of which we are made. My party and I are such Republicans.

He quotes as a mark of maturity in the Republic the change suggested in Article 3 of the Constitution by an All Party Committee of the Oireachtas in 1967. The new form of words was: "The Irish nation hereby proclaims its firm will that its territory be re-united in harmony and brotherly affection between all Irishmen." And he notes with satisfaction that the recommendation was signed by Lemass — Lemass who had fought in the GPO in 1916, had served in the most important ministries in the land, had broken old moulds when as Taoiseach in 1965 he visited Terence O'Neill, then Prime Minister at Stormont and gave hope of ushering in a new era in Irish politics.

Sean Lemass had no identity crisis about his Irishness, his Republicanism or his leadership role. He saw that people came before crude concepts based on territorial acquisition.

Inviting Unionists to meet him and his colleagues, he said:

Without such dialogue the immediate prospects for life in this community looks bleak. For my part I want to say that our door is always open. The path of dialogue may be tedious, slow and at times frustrating but all who believe in constitutional politics must see it as the only realistic option.

When Haughey accused the Progressive Democrats of making a deal to keep the Coalition Government in power, O'Malley replied with what amounted to a definition of Haughey's standards:

He makes the mistake of believing that others will act as he would. His experience of political deals for short-term party advantage is considerable, but he need not fear that the Progressive Democrats will adopt his principles in such matters.

But his most constant theme is the exercise of choice, whether that applies to social issues, personal spending power or public expenditure:

There are many, politicians and commentators alike, who are paralysed by the scale and extent of our present [financial] difficulties into believing that nothing can be done. They say we are a small economy and the Government has little discretion — "but what can the Government do?" But there is discretion. It is exercised at every Cabinet meeting. It is evident in every budget and every estimate for every Department. Governments can set rates of pay, the range and rate of welfare entitlements, the charges for public services, the range and level of grants to be paid to different sectors, the level of resources given to policing the tax and welfare systems. All these are discretionary matters. They are not set by some immutable economic laws. They result from choices. Choices made by Government. There are choices. We are saying: let us exercise them.

Choice and change: O'Malley believes that that is what the electorate wants and, with visionary leadership, he can help to provide both.

Facing the Future

WITHIN MONTHS OF his arrival as leader of a new party, Des O'Malley had to begin preparing for a General Election. It was a baptism of fire he could have done without, as he could have done without being plunged into the Department of Justice two years after his arrival in the Dáil. No sooner had the Progressive Democrats begun to organise in the constituencies than they were being challenged to produce policy documents in every area of government. In some cases, they were challenged to produce policies where the established parties had none. In the referendum, which was held less than seven months after

113

their foundation, putative allies complained of their lack of organisation on the ground. Throughout the summer and early autumn, they watched in alarm as the Government teetered nervously, then recovered sufficiently to win a vote of confidence in the Dáil.

There is no such thing as an unimportant General Election, but some are undoubtedly more important than others. 1932 changed the course of Irish history; only the participants can now remember the contests of, say, 1943 or 1944. The election with which the PDs were faced was more likely, for a variety of reasons, to resemble 1932. And, for a time, it looked as though they might hold the balance of power: not only were policies demanded, it was essential to devise an electoral strategy as well.

In the face of such challenges, it was a tribute to O'Malley and his colleagues that they should have consolidated their column of support in the opinion polls, after a period in which commentators and opponents were prepared to write them off. They had weathered the storm of high and unexpected popularity and a prominence which even their most optimistic supporters would scarcely have predicted. And they had shown that they were capable of fighting back when that popularity had slumped to the point where it was generally believed that they would be lucky to hold the Dáil seats they had.

At his and the party's high point, O'Malley cheerfully admitted that there would be fluctuations in the level of support. Even as the annual conference cheered his achievement, he insisted that the requirements of political leadership meant that popularity for its own sake should never be their aim. When the first policy document on taxation was published, it was accompanied by detailed information about the cuts in public spending that would be needed to ensure that tax relief might be provided. No one had any doubt that this would lead to controversy, raising again the accusation that the welfare system was going to suffer; and the promise of a bitter debate was well and truly fulfilled. It was the first substantial argument of the General Election campaign.

That so much attention should have been focussed on O'Malley as leader was inevitable, however he tried to dismiss the assumptions that a one-man party was either possible or desirable. The elections of the Eighties had been fought in presidential style and, whether he liked it or not, he was cast in a role which failed to distinguish between party and leader. Which meant that the pressure on him was greater than he had endured in Justice or during the frustrated challenges to Haughey, though of a different kind. Now, at least, he was master of his own ship and, to a much greater extent than before, capable of determining what its course should be.

He still bore some of the scars of the old campaigns, which were exposed from time to time as hints of suspicion, flashes of anger. He is still capable of spotting a conspiracy a mile away. More often, nowadays, one of the most ordered minds and sharpest intellects in Irish politics is busy with problems that he considers as urgent as those of the Fifties or early Seventies. His ability is justly recognised, grudgingly by some of those opponents who can see no farther than their political noses, with something approaching adulation by his admirers. His reactions to both are slightly quizzical, just a bit detached. Because he has never aspired to being anyone's hero, he considers himself to be nobody's fool.

The Bodhrán Makers
by John B. Keane

"This powerful and poignant novel provides John B. Keane with a passport to the highest levels of Irish literature ... an important and valuable book which must be read by all who love Ireland."
– The Irish Press

"A rivetting read ... It will hold the reader until the last glowing embers of the turf fire die away."
– The Belfast Telegraph

"The book has everything, humour, romance and tragedy. There is an abundance of rich characters. John B. Keane can paint the real-life picture of rural Ireland just as Thomas Hardy captured English rural life. *The Bodhran Makers* is sheer enjoyment to read and it would make a wonderful film. That man Keane is a genius."
— Andersonstown News

"A full 350 pages of sheer enjoyment ... totally captivating."
— Northern Standard

"A wonderful, wonderful book."
– Gay Byrne, The Late Late Show

350 pages; paperback £4.95   **ISBN 0 86322 085 1**

The Politics of Irish Freedom
Gerry Adams

President of Sinn Féin and Westminster MP for West Belfast, Gerry Adams offers his own view of the political questions raised in Ireland during the last twenty years. He describes the nature of modern republicanism and the changes it has undergone in the course of the protracted political crisis in Northern Ireland.

As was written of his previous book, *Falls Memories*, "Adams is an eloquent man who can put a good case for his politics." *(Tribune)*

192 pages; paperback £3.95; ISBN 0 86322 084 3

One Girl's War
Joan Miller

One Girl's War is a fascinating memoir from the heart of the world of intelligence operations in wartime Britain, when Joan Miller was personal assistant to Maxwell Knight, chief of M15.

160 pages; hardback £9.95; ISBN 086322 081 9

Ireland in Crisis, a study in capitalist, colonial undevelopment.
Raymond Crotty

"A profoundly original contribution to economic history. . . . His diagnosis of our crisis is compelling. . . . The kind of intellectual urgency one finds only in the writings of the economic Greats. This book is a landmark in Irish social science and contains an implicit research agenda breathtaking in scope." *(Irish Independent)*

304 pages; paperback £12.50; ISBN 0 86322 083 5